REDISCOVERING EARTH

REDISCOVERING EARTH

TEN DIALOGUES ON THE FUTURE OF NATURE

CONVERSATIONS WITH ANDERS DUNKER

OR Books
New York · London

All rights information: rights@orbooks.com
Visit our website at www.orbooks.com
First printing 2020

Published by OR Books, New York and London

© 2021 Anders Dunker

All rights reserved. No part of this book may be reproduced or transmitted in any form or by any means, electronic or mechanical, including photocopy, recording, or any information storage retrieval system, without permission in writing from the publisher, except brief passages for review purposes.

Library of Congress Cataloging-in-Publication Data: A catalog record for this book is available from the Library of Congress.

Typeset by Lapiz Digital Services. Printed by Bookmobile, USA, and CPI, UK.

paperback ISBN 978-1-68219-508-6 • ebook ISBN 978-1-68219-296-2

For Annalisa–with gratitude for all of your love and support.

TABLE OF CONTENTS

The Environmental Crisis as Learning Process
    Anders Dunker   1

The Rediscovery of the Earth
    with Bruno Latour   9

The Meaning of Natural Life
    with Ursula K. Heise   27

Entering a Vaster History
    with Dipesh Chakrabarty   45

On Crisis, Collapse, and Tikopians
    with Jared Diamond   73

Restarting the World System
    with Bernard Stiegler   93

The Plants, the Planet, and Us
    with Sandra Díaz   119

Changing the Human Game
    with Bill McKibben   137

Death by Unnatural Causes
    with Vandana Shiva   161

Climate Responsibility and Moral Evasion
with Clive Hamilton 177

Taking the Temperature of the Future
with Kim Stanley Robinson 199

Acknowledgments 215

THE ENVIRONMENTAL CRISIS AS LEARNING PROCESS

Anders Dunker

Our experience of what we call nature is in many ways confusing. When we look around, familiar places appear to be much the same as they always were. Wild tracts of land and the open sea feel timeless and unchanging. At the same time, we are warned and reminded that this impression depends largely on how observant we choose to be, on how well we know the past, and on how much we really understand about the changes that are upon us. Scientists tell us that more than three quarters of flying insects in Europe have disappeared, that the permafrost is rapidly thawing, and that coral reefs are dying off, leaving only bleached ruins. And yet, in most places, things appear normal. So far, it still seems entirely possible to convince oneself that the world will just carry on.

People living on sinking atolls tell a very different story, and the media serves to increase our awareness of global events and make us ever more citizens of Earth, witnesses to and participants in an unfolding drama. We glimpse, but fail to take in, the enormity and the fine-grained detail of this supercluster of events. One of the aims of this book is to offer perspectives on the environmental crisis from theorists, scientists, and thinkers who, for a long time, have devoted their attention to what is happening. Even if we are all witnesses, informed testimonials can help deepen our understanding of the overwhelming event we find ourselves playing a part in.

If we live in a terrifying time, it is also one that can be sobering and even energizing, precisely because absolutely everything is at stake—a time when we need to discover and invent new ways of living, new ways of understanding nature and ourselves. Life, and our understanding of it, is radically changing. Civilization must change with it.

Responding to such a collective threat will require a collective effort—as we have seen with the recent COVID-19 pandemic. A collective threat puts us in the same boat and can become a story of collective overcoming—but as the history of shipwrecks tells us, a sense of community can also crack under pressure, making the crisis a cause of strife and division. If the COVID-19 crisis has made many of us reflect on climate change and the environment, it is not only because both crises affect humanity at large—or because tackling them will require good science and a resolute trust in it; it is also because they are both urgent and incredibly complex. The causes and effects of the pandemic are multifaceted, involving wild animals, infrastructure, mutation rates, as well as bodily and social immune systems. The same goes for ecological and geophysical problems: both the causes and effects of perilous changes are staggeringly intricate, weaving our everyday lives together with stories of glaciers and ocean currents, combustion machines and colonialization, insects and the Internet. In a global pandemic, the time afforded for learning is relatively short. With climate, the game is longer, but we may have to learn from our mistakes before we experience their consequences firsthand.

The word "unsustainable" hangs over our heads like the Sword of Damocles. Yet most of us, most of the time, remain unconcerned. Those whose concern has become an awakening, take to the streets to awaken others in turn—and precisely because the problems are more than technical, movements like Extinction Rebellion have acted out the existential and emotional sides of what is increasingly becoming a moral drama. Protests dramatize the conflict, but the genuine battleground is in the lawmaker's arena more than anywhere else, where the priority given to the environment and the climate crisis is still despairingly low. Our knowledge has failed to create action, and what action has been taken has failed to make significant change. The message behind the wave of school strikes led by Greta Thunberg is simple enough and shouldn't be criticized for being so: we must take action. But if taking action was simple, we would have done it already.

We need to understand the deeper reasons why we still don't enact serious change and explore the internal and external obstacles. The urgent need to act is in fact accompanied by an urgent need to talk, discuss, think, and fathom. Talk and deliberation must not replace action, but it must certainly accompany it, as we commence a process of personal and cultural transformation. The pedagogic commonplace of "learning to learn" must be supplemented with the principle of "learning fast how to learn fast."

In all these conversations, the gap between what we humans know and what we do surfaces over and over as a fatal conundrum. Discussions of this problem go back to antiquity, to Plato and Aristotle, whose ethical observations remain relevant to a modern-day environmental perspective. Both Plato and Aristotle contend that we do ourselves a disservice if we simply conclude that we are weak-willed, or that moral knowledge doesn't compel moral action. The solution to what contemporary psychology calls "cognitive dissonance" lies in the gradual deepening of one's understanding, working our knowledge into our lives through continued practice, beyond restating facts and moral imperatives to ourselves and each other.

Wisdom, the basic sense of knowing how to live well, can no longer be understood in a traditional way. As our conception of the good life becomes determined by long-term survival and thriving for humans and nonhumans, our culture must be revised, old ways rediscovered, new ways invented. We must constantly reassess and find out which things we can't keep doing and which we can and must do instead. Who and what needs to change in which respects? Ours is a great age of cultural reinvention.

While the natural sciences reveal the crucial facts of the environmental crisis, the struggle to mitigate it takes place in culture. Our cultural inertia can hardly be explained by the laws of physics. The selection of writers and thinkers collected in this book all attempt to transplant discoveries from the domain of the natural sciences to a broader cultural field. For new insights to take root in culture at large, they need to be integrated with our other systems of knowledge, and be nourished by insights and considerations from anthropology, history, philosophy, and literature.

Our learning process today is not only personal, but collective, and consists in "ecologizing mankind," to borrow a phrase from the French thinker Edgar Morin. More than anything, an ecological mentality requires an expansion of our sphere of interest. We must think bigger—stretching our mental and practical participation in the world out through space and time, geographically and historically.

Thinking of the environmental crisis as a learning process means hoping for the type of historical development Kant envisaged over two hundred years ago—not a naïve faith in linear progress, but one that mixes faith in moral progress with a realistic understanding of humankind's grave missteps and obvious shortcomings. This means we must be prepared to see contradictions, and even the gravest transgressions, as steps on the path to ever increasing enlightenment—detours to maturity. Those who study the past know full well that it is frequently littered with hopeless regression and all kinds of lamentable repetition. Still, we shouldn't be misled by Hegel's sardonic quip that the only thing that history teaches us is that we never learn from history. Even if all of our institutions and cultures are, and must be, geared for repetition in order to secure their own perpetuation, thus passing on old and often dysfunctional patterns, and even if old mistakes are complemented by new and unexpected missteps, it still holds true that all of our institutions—indeed, our whole culture—has evolved through a progressive learning process. We are constantly changing our society to tackle new problems, gathering knowledge and communicating with each other faster than ever before. Legal systems are beginning to criminalize environmental destruction. School systems are teaching climate science. Political institutions are being built to tackle new challenges.

There is no way for climate change and the sixth extinction to be solved or mitigated, except through human dialogue, resulting in new laws, values, knowledge, and reason. It is my hope that the following series of conversations will bring these topics to life for readers. They can be read as interviews or as journalistic presentations of theoretical thought. They can also be read as dialogues, apropos of an ancient philosophical genre.

At its best, a dialogue not only transmits knowledge, but also dramatizes reactions, associations—an imperfect and often inconclusive search for answers, understanding in its lived form. The aim must be to replace our sense of panic with measured understanding and the courage to act. Philosophical questioning involves making the space and taking the time to think things over calmly from a certain distance, allowing us to make even the most pressing problems into objects of interest and wonder as we seek an overarching point of view and insight into what is most hidden. The thinkers I have chosen for these conversations have in common the capacity to transmit wonder and excitement toward the power of nature, even in light of pressing problems. Being critical thinkers, they all have a share of what Gramsci called the "pessimism of the intellect," but they also demonstrate its counterpart: an "optimism of the will"—that is, hope.

Hope presupposes a future into which it can be projected, and the crisis, many of the voices in this little book point out, is no longer ahead of us—we are in the middle of it. The massive loss of coral reefs worldwide, by and far irrevocable, reminds us of the monumental gravity of our moment. The temperature rise of the atmosphere is staggering, and deadly heatwaves and violent storms are just around the corner. Still, granted how much worse it might all get very soon, and given how much we still have to lose—and thus to fight for—we still live in a paradise, a living planet that remains very much intact. A minimalist utopian vision is the simplest hope that everything can somehow still go on, that global society doesn't have to collapse all together, and that most of nature really does have a future.

Should we dare to posit a loftier hope for the future, it would have to be that we manage to live up to the gravity of the moment and get back to Earth—rediscover Earth—so that handling environmental challenges becomes our central ambition. Our response to the environmental crisis can become a full-scale transformation that does not irresolutely unfold with tired reluctance, but emerges as a wholehearted and concerted effort—mustering up an untold imagination and a courage to think not only extremely big, but big enough. There is still hope that the crisis may unite us and not divide us. If we are to believe in human civilization at all, we must also have the courage to think of its continuation for tens of thousands of years. If civilization can be made sustainable, there is practically an eternity ahead of us.

THE REDISCOVERY OF THE EARTH

with Bruno Latour

Bruno Latour (b. 1947) is one of the most respected science studies theorists of our time. His interdisciplinary works are alternately described as sociology of science, philosophy, and anthropology. Latour is often considered the foremost representative of "actor-network theory," abbreviated as ANT. In his famous scientific historical analysis *We Have Never Been Modern* (1991), Latour lays out a fundamental critique of the distinction between man and nature.

In recent books, Latour has increasingly turned his attention to the politics of nature and climate science. In *The Politics of Nature*, he examines the representation of nature in politics and explores the political implications of our problematic distinction between nature and society. His book *Facing Gaia: Eight Lectures on the New Climatic Regime* (2015) forms much of the basis for the below conversation.

Prompted by the Trump administration's decision to exit the Paris Agreement, Latour wrote the pamphlet *Down to Earth: Politics in the New Climatic Regime* (2017), where he examines world politics in relation to the climate crisis and our reactions to it. To make mankind's ecological living conditions a part of our political consciousness, Latour proposes a radical rethinking of shared territories and the space we inhabit.

Anders Dunker (AD): In your book *Paris: Ville Invisible* (Paris, The Invisible City), published in 1998, you try to show how difficult it really is to see Paris. You argue that the city cannot be genuinely appreciated by means of a map or panoramic view because seeing into the city must also include perception of the society inhabiting it—and "society" in this sense is almost impossible to make visible in its entirety. Would you say that your recently released book, *Facing Gaia* (2017), is a similar attempt to describe Earth as the invisible planet?

Bruno Latour (BL): Panoramas are deceptive. Accordingly, photographs of the earth seen from space can be deceptive. They provide a false notion of unity and oversight, which does not contribute to our understanding of the reality of our situation. When you see the earth from afar, you are not seeing it from any place you would actually ever be, unless you're an astronaut. It is not true, as people say, that these images show us how fragile the planet is out there in the universe. We understand the earth's fragility only when we consider ecological and geophysical processes through myriad encounters and investigations. We really ought to improve the way we go about understanding our world, because when we adopt a typical "cosmic" point of view—when we take a "planetary" perspective on Earth—the diverse people and lifeforms of our world become totally negligible.

AD: And "nature," in its widest conception, includes things like black holes, intergalactic stellar clouds, etc. . . . entities of an altogether different kind than the fragile and complex ecosystems here on Earth.

BL: That is precisely why the concept of "nature" is too wide. We don't live in nature; we live in a critical zone.

AD: What, exactly, is this "critical zone"? Are we talking about the biosphere?

BL: I like the concept of a critical zone because it is a reminder that the zone where life thrives is wafer thin, like a layer of varnish covering the globe. We are not so much living upon the globe as we are living inside this thin life-sustaining layer.

"Biosphere" is a term derived from the Swiss geologist Eduard Suess, which was developed further by the Soviet Russian bio- and geochemist Vladimir Vernadskij. We can define the biosphere, in short, as the part of the earth and the atmosphere in which there is life and as the totality of relationships between all the living beings and organisms we find there—earthworms, plants, fungi, and so on. In other words, the biosphere can be understood as the sum of all ecosystems on the planet. The critical zone is more of a geophysical or geochemical concept—it is bio-geochemical. Here, too, we do well to draw interesting connecting lines with the circuit of H_2O, or sulfur and atmospheric gases, and to the interrelation of all organisms. This zone also holds all the things that have been modified by life forms in the atmosphere. This is how we can say that the critical zone is synonymous with Gaia—the British naturalist James Lovelock uses this term in his well-known hypothesis. But the central point is that organisms have modified themselves and their surroundings and have actually brought forth the critical zone that we all depend on.

AD: In criticizing the concept of nature, there seems always to be a risk that such a move will be seen as an attack on nature itself. The concept of the post-natural, or the end of nature, used by the American activist Bill McKibben, has led some people to argue, "Nature is nothing but a construction so there is no need to protect it." Or, alternatively, "All of nature is conditioned by humans, so there is no use trying to protect it." Do we really no longer have a need for the cherished concept of nature?

BL: It may be the case that without the old concept of nature, wilderness and various ecosystems will be left unprotected: They risk being reduced to mere resources. This is what Heidegger called *gestell*, something that can be used and exploited for whatever intrinsic value and dignity it might be said to possess. But the irony is that precisely the old conception of nature has caused this reduction, since it is the distinction between humans and nature that reduces nature to something purely manipulable, something "objective" and "material," whereas only humans are granted real agency. In this sense, the struggle to protect nature is misguided. Anything we do, or can possibly do, implies obeying the laws of nature—even when we destroy other life forms and habitats. Because of this, I prefer to speak about Gaia. When you speak about Gaia, you will realize that an enormous number of agents—that is, acting parties—are interconnected. Then you can also begin to give up on the simplification of this multifarious diversity with concepts like "objectivity" and "materiality." This is why I have never really understood the argument that it is risky or irresponsible to give up the concept of nature. Yet, it is, of course, possible to misunderstand me and take away that there is no nature because everything is artificial, but in the Anthropocene, which is precisely the epoch where even geophysical systems are influenced by humans, it is also difficult to find places that are natural in the old fashioned sense. In this respect the post-natural is a fact we have to learn to live with if nature is to signify wilderness.

AD: The question of how far we can go in manipulating nature comes up in discussions about what is referred to as climate engineering or geoengineering—direct technological interventions in the atmosphere. Such solutions are popular among ecomodernists, but you seem ambivalent?

BL: I draw a line between geoengineering and planetary design. The argument is taken from the German philosopher Peter Sloterdijk, who says that we have never lived on the "outside"—we always live in some contained interior or other. That we always are inside seems obvious, but it is constantly forgotten. The new aspect of the situation is that we will need to build new and artificial spaces, a kind of protective interiority for humanity. This is a very general task, to secure humanity's lifeworld, so to speak. If this task also involves the air-conditioning of the planet, we can say that we are already are doing it, albeit in a very bad way, because we are simply turning up the heat instead of cooling things down. In any case, being able to influence things on that kind of scale is not just something we imagine, it's something we're already doing. We are truly like Prometheus, stealing fire from the gods. When I am ambivalent about geoengineering, which will primarily involve changes in the upper atmosphere by releasing sulfur particles and so on, then it is because I have read up on the subject and have understood how little we know about the possible consequences of such interventions. I am a fearsome, not to say a terrified Prometheus, when it comes to interventions of this kind.

AD: Does our capacity to make such changes reinforce the narrative of strong human agency, wherein our atmosphere and ecosystems are yet again seen as manipulable objects?

BL: I am haunted by these questions. My friend, the Australian climate thinker Clive Hamilton, has told me: "Bruno, you may be right that humans are not the only active party, that there are endless nonhuman-like organisms interacting together with humans, but on a more strategic level you are mistaken: Humankind is back with full strength." I, and all of my friends in the humanities and social sciences, hate the idea that "Anthropocene" means we take control of the planet. If the representative of humanity is Donald Trump or Monsanto-Bayer, the multinational company producing genetically modified organisms, then we are on thin ice. If, however, a government like that of Norway was to represent humanity, we might be less frightened—but still . . . we won't be completely reassured. Either way, it is a strong argument: Yes, humankind is back. Yes, the redesign of the planet has already begun. How are we going to do good rather than bad? At the same time, we will not have total control over the environment. We know it is impossible. Our knowledge is too limited. In any case, it would be disastrous to give such power to anyone, especially Monsanto or Trump, with more influence than geochemists and glaciologists. And we cannot be divided if we are to make decisions about climatic intervention.

AD: Are we right to say that we are responsible for the problems we have caused, so that refraining from action is likewise unthinkable, either through cuts in CO_2 emissions or more extreme actions?

BL: Yes. The situation is very different from, for instance, the risk of thermonuclear war. In that case, we are always talking about different scenarios of what might happen. With the climate, we are talking about something that has already happened. We have already acted like geoengineers. But how do we relate morally, ex post facto, to past actions in light of new and evolving standards. It's a tricky ethical question.

If we take action, for instance, by keeping the global temperature under 1.5 degrees above preindustrial levels, which doesn't seem very doable at all, we will engage in geoengineering. If we don't act, that is also our choice and responsibility. In both cases, humanity is in a position of command. But all my friends and colleagues from anthropology and other subjects, where one is concerned with the nonhuman and of the Other, are tremendously opposed to this way of thinking. They would prefer if humans had no control nor power to decide. But this also entails closing your eyes to our moral responsibilities. This is by no means easy.

AD: So what is the solution?

BL: My solution, these days, is to search for a new definition of what it means to live on Earth. That means understanding the earth as something other and more than total globalization. We must find a way to relate to an even bigger situation and ask how we are to position ourselves. But then we easily become designers embarking on planetary design...

AD: Which is also a redesign of society?

BL: We must rethink society, the commons, the cities. We have failed to act. Or, alternatively, we are part of a collective action that keeps playing itself out and that has gradually transported us to another stage. In certain ways it is like being at war, yet it is different. In a war, you can always stop.

AD: The question of inaction, of how we can know about climate issues and still not do anything about it, is a problem many people are trying to solve. You have suggested that this lack of action has religious roots.

BL: Yes, I think that without religion, this is completely incomprehensible. If we didn't have religious systems of belief, we would have acted. The problem is that we perceive ourselves as invulnerable, as if we were already saved. We live, think, and feel as if nothing could hurt us anymore. Many people think that we deserve modernization. The Kingdom of God, in its secular version—that is, wealth and abundance—is our *right*. We are already in the promised land. Why should we then leave this promised land?! To wander the desert again searching for another?! It's unthinkable! Living apocalyptically does not, of course, mean leaving an apocalypse behind, but really to live in the end times.

AD: What does that mean—living in the end times?

BL: We must distinguish the apocalypse from the special effects, from Hollywood's depictions of the end of the world. The fires that have ravaged around Hollywood are much more terrifying than any special effects. The end of the world is becoming literal, and at the same time there is a lack of apocalyptic imagination. We live as if we are safe, in a kind of timeless paradise of prosperity, while we are in fact, in very concrete ways, about to destroy the planet.

AD: Are there no other ways forward than either lifting our spirits through escapism or confronting the terror without hope? Can we live heroically in the end times, even if it is in a completely pragmatic way. If we first describe the situation and then ask what kind of people and attitudes are required, can we not then also attempt to assume these roles?

BL: This is what I'm trying, in a sense, to figure out: What are the appropriate political attitudes, and what personality archetypes does the situation call forth? This is why I talk about *Earthlings* or the Earthbound. If we need to be heroic, then let us be heroic! I seek out this attitude in my last book, *Down to Earth*. It is not so much about designing the proper people or of deciding what moral equipment we will need, as it is about finding out where we need to be landing. This task is different from that posed by earlier schools of ecology, who took nature for granted, as something under our feet that we could find our way back to and to which we might reconnect. I have great respect for Arne Naess and deep ecology, but we have to think all together differently. "Nature" is not the place we will land. "Nature" has been one of the sources of our indifference not for nature lovers, of course, but for countless others for whom nature has become the name of a kind of object that humans can manipulate freely. The earth is something completely different than nature. The earth—and this is the heroic aspect—is a promised land, so to speak; at the same time it is the place we need to land after modernity's lofty dreams of eternal growth.

AD: At the same time unrealistic and extremist attitudes abound in politics. Why is the ecological crisis polarizing us, even if we all know we share one planet and one atmosphere?

BL: There are many people who tend toward extreme modernization—more and more they are becoming eccentric figures—hypermodern billionaires in Silicon Valley or Los Angeles who promote space travel to Mars, faster and faster airplanes, genetic engineering, and autonomous robots. The modern imagination has become baroque and extravagant and shows minimal concern for the billions of people who will not benefit from the so-called progress. On the other hand, you have nationalist extremists, even more confrontational and hateful, holding on to the impossible dream of nostalgic provincialism, even as we cross the threshold of the Anthropocene. This is where Trump is interesting.

AD: In *Down to Earth*, you write about Trump being a symptom of denial not only of the climate crisis, but of our shared global situation as such?

BL: The interesting thing is that Trump stands for something entirely new. He tries to unite two impossible extremes. He wants to take financial capitalism to its extreme while pining after an old national homeland:

the great old America of yesteryear. My argument, which I can't prove, but which I make efforts to present in the book, is that this is only possibly through climate denial. The withdrawal from the climate agreement proves that climate is the new geopolitics—an attitude that may not be new but was never before demonstrated so explicitly. All of the world's nations have tried to greenwash their economies. Only Trump says: "You have a climate problem—we don't." The withdrawal is as a kind of declaration of war and a sign that we have entered a kind of global civil war.

AD: So even this state of a global civil war doesn't rest on a clear conception of a shared situation?

BL: No conservative thinker would say: "You have an ecological crisis—we don't." This contradicts the idea of nature as common property, the shared condition of our existence. We are searching for a new frontier, but we don't really know what that means. Migration is also highly relevant here because it changes the landscape both for arriving migrants and the communities that receive them. Deregulated globalization means that everything circulates throughout. We are dealing with what German political thinker Carl Schmitt called *raumordnungskrieg*—a conflict concerning the territorial organization of the world. It is a fruitful concept, because this is exactly where we are now: migration, dwindling wildlife populations, wolves versus farmers, ecology, oil interests...

AD: And various players are defining "territory," "citizenship," and "borders" in different ways.

BL: In a certain respect, even the concept of territory is being redefined. Formerly, a territory was primarily something legal and juridical, something flat and two-dimensional, something connected to historical roots embodied by the graveyards of one's ancestors. Now, from a number of sources, a new interest in territories has emerged, but it is understood very differently: not as something two-dimensional, but as something thick and layered. A number of territories overlap in any given place. Artists, characteristically ahead of things, picked up the zeitgeist and are currently exploring with soils, earthworms, humus, and growth zones. In England, social scientists have conducted a study of soils—something which would have been seen as unthinkable not long ago. Gradually, territory is becoming something more material, something different than mere geographical regions on a map. Even permaculture has become a fad: gardening and slow food are moving into mainstream culture and politics.

AD: For nature to really be included in politics, I suppose you would need a great number of people speaking up on behalf of other creatures. Are there enough people who care about the voiceless? How can we mobilize people to do something, for instance, about, the loss of flying insects in Europe, recently measured to have dropped by 80 percent?

BL: That depends, but this is precisely what it means to be in a state of war. The size of your army is vital to your success in battle: how many battalions can you assemble? Things can change very fast. We must take care not to deduce our conclusions from what is intellectually plausible, but rather pay heed to what is happening in the real world. You can look at what activists are actually doing by allying themselves with scientists and working with farmers and fishermen. In this way, a multitude of new experiences come to light and start to change the idea of political representation. How much more important it becomes to describe the world in new ways, because only through new descriptions can we get a grip on what's going on. If you want to examine the drop in insect populations, you must ask "Where are the insects disappearing from?" It may not be easy to imagine a group protesting in order to regain all the insects that used to plaster their windshields just ten or twenty years ago. Yet this must be our goal. We want dirty windshields once more! This is a difficult cause in which to get people engaged because of what we call "shifting baseline syndrome." When fewer and fewer bugs are present, people quickly get used to it and experience it as new normal. This is a very depressing piece of psychology.

When I was young, we had to wash the windshield all the time. Young people don't miss insects because they have never experienced them. Describing the world in new ways is, to me, a novel way to change politics—a political movement in both senses, wherein new descriptions lead to a full-scale reorientation. In this way we can, for example, suddenly become passionate about insects we used to see as a nuisance.

AD: Historically, the age of discovery is over. Are we none the less in a new age—an age of rediscovery—that can lift our spirits and propel us past the nagging feelings of tragedy?

BL: Well, it is my way of being optimistic. It is my way of not taking part in the sense of doom. Scientifically and technically, it is perfectly rational to be a pessimist, but I don't think it makes much sense politically. Optimism has nothing to do with technoscience—DNA plus cognitive science plus robots plus outer space. Instead it is connected with exploring the world we thought we knew. I will borrow the term from you and call our time period an age of rediscovery, even if it is grandiose. What we call local has quite a different meaning in relation to Gaia than it previously had. It now has many different dimensions. The rediscovery of a place is in some ways a cliché—since ecologists have been talking about the same thing for years—but this concept also leads to a different way of framing the world, it leads to another geometry, so to speak. Water gets another meaning. Ice gets another meaning. Industry is considered in relation to the amount of CO_2 in the atmosphere. We see things in new ways. Antibiotics have a different kind of globalization than weeds, for example.

AD: Traditionally, the concept of the local has had a flavor of subjectivity—existence circumscribed by the immediate horizon—in contrast to the scientific gaze, which purports to see everything as if from outer space?

BL: And here lies the error. The local is objective. The gaze from inside the critical zone is completely objective, it is just objective in a different way. What we see is real, but this reality only becomes visible if we learn what different parties are up to, what they need, what they want, what they can accomplish.

AD: But when we see things from the inside and rediscover our surroundings as a mesh of territories, the question arises: from whose perspective should we see these territories? There is obviously a myriad of lifeforms, both human and nonhuman, with different and potentially conflicting interests. Doesn't this beg the question of negotiating the right to exist—to be what one is?

BL: For me, the decisive question is this: When one talks about one's territory, does this territory contain other beings or not? If you define other beings as part of your territory, defending your territory also means defending insects and birds. So there are those who belong to *society*, as my countryman Émile Durkheim defined it: that is, to an exclusively *human* society. Such people resist an inclusive definition of their territory containing insects and birds. In this way, there is a struggle between different kinds of cosmopolitanism—or cosmopolitics, if you like—which isn't really that different from politics as ordinarily conceived. In Norway, for instance, youth protesters are attacking oil interests drilling in the Arctic and suing the government. They are using the law to say, "What you are doing is wrong and constitutes an attack on all of us." This is politics the way politics has always been conducted. We tend to distinguish between ecological issues and political issues, but this is both strange and mistaken—they are essentially the same.

AD: So rather than speaking about the sixth extinction and global warming in general, we must discover the battleground in our immediate vicinity?

BL: We are drowning in horrible information about global ecological disaster. The net result is paralysis. Some time ago, *Le Monde* published a warning about climate change signed by 15,000 scientists in big letters on the front page. But what do you do with that? Where do you go from there? People are left with a feeling of helplessness. This is where many environmental thinkers make a mistake. They preach about the end of the world but fail to understand the drama in multiple dimensions. When we only emphasize the tragic side of things, we end up instead in a kind of pedagogic tragedy. It is important to remember the comedic side of things, which is more affirmative. I have collaborated in writing a play about Gaia that is a tragicomedy. Comedy is a way to avoid the rigidity of tragedy. We don't need more pedagogic tragedies, but rather to start lively debates and to stage possibilities for reality in new ways. Comedy, drama, exhibitions, performances—this is our only way of freeing ourselves from the sense of helplessness.

AD: What about politics? Historian of technology and the environment Jean Baptiste Fressoz has said that we have ended up seeing nature as malleable and capitalist society as virtually immoveable. Is there nothing we can do to change the system?

BL: This is actually the topic of a new book by a colleague of mine, Michel Callon [*L'Emprise des marchés: Comprendre leur fonctionnement pour pouvoir les changer* (2017)]. He writes about the economy from the same perspective. As it turns out, the economy, seen from a sociological and anthropological angle, is much more flexible than people assume. The Left's obsession with the "system"—and the seeming impossibility of changing it—is ultimately counterproductive. It prevents critics from perceiving the diverse multitude of economic practices.

AD: So has the critique of capitalism become no more than a melancholy investigation of why the Left is condemned to lose the battle?

BL: Yes, it is typically a radical position fascinated with the enemy.

AD: You have sometimes suggested that by making plans for green economies, we risk adding another agenda that merely competes for attention. You seem skeptical about the idea of economizing ecology. Should we, instead, ecologize the economy?

BL: There are many people who try to economize ecology in interesting ways. In the past, I have partly been a victim of my anticapitalistic tendencies, also under the influence of friends. Callon's book has made me think differently. I think your formulation is correct. The point is to ecologize the economy because the economy is already so complex. Capitalism is not a map of our economy, but a mode of navigating it that also contributes to how it takes shape. There is a beautiful line, by the French sociologist Gabriel Tarde, saying that economists are so convinced by the ideology of the scientific revolution that, when they are faced with a problem that is close at hand, they aim to see it from as far away as possible and end up seeing nothing at all. They think, for instance, that they are imitating astronomy. Despite the fact that an astronomer would probably sell his own mother for the chance to see cosmic phenomena up close. It is only lack of access to what lies in front of their noses that necessitates such a faraway perspective and that engenders their reliance on diagrams and instruments. Here we come back to my book about Paris. For if we could see the economy like we see the city of Paris, we would immediately identify all the openings, roads, connections, and possible maneuvers that we fail to consider when we simply describe it as capitalistic. If we regard the economy as an ecology, we understand that a change in cosmology, cosmography or whatever you want to call it, makes a huge difference. Such a perspective is both cartographical and political at the same time.

THE MEANING OF NATURAL LIFE

with Ursula K. Heise

Ursula K. Heise (b. 1960) is a German-born theorist, currently Professor of English and Chair of the Department of English at UCLA. Her main field of research is the environmental humanities, which connects the natural sciences and political ecology with disciplines in the humanities, such as cultural history, literary studies, and critical theory. Heise specializes in the theory and practice of environmental narrative from a cross-cultural perspective.

In her book *Sense of Place and Sense of Planet: The Environmental Imagination of the Global* (2008), Heise analyzes how environmental thinkers and writers have envisioned the relationship between local places, regions, and the planet as a whole from the 1960s to the present. She connects theories of globalization and of local and global perceptions of risk with the analysis of cultural artifacts as well as images and texts across media to argue that a sense of planet or "eco-cosmopolitanism" is as crucial for environmental justice today as a sense of place.

In *Imagining Extinction: The Cultural Meanings of Endangered Species* (2016), Heise explores what makes us care about endangered animal and plant species, as well as species that have already been lost. She focuses on the stories that are told about endangered species across different cultures and analyzes how they are linked to the stories particular communities tell about their own past, present, and futures. Besides stories told through paintings, photographs, films, and literary works, the book analyzes narratives of endangered species as they emerge in biodiversity databases and endangered species laws. These narratives form part of the larger context of conflicts and convergences between conservationists and animal rights activists, on one hand, and between conservationists and environmental justice advocates, on the other – both engagements that form part of multispecies justice in the Anthropocene.

In her preface to *The Routledge Companion to the Environmental Humanities* (2017), Heise emphasizes that environmental problems are fundamentally issues of society, history, and culture rather than problems of science and technology. Rather than merely contributing to the analysis of the "cultural dimensions of environmental crisis," the humanities ae therefore fundamental for the understanding of how different cultural communities engage with ecological crises today, and for devising solutions that work in divergent cultural frameworks.

Anders Dunker: When we talk about the meaning of life, we seem to take for granted that we talk about human life. In your book *Imagining Extinction: The Cultural Meanings of Endangered Species*, you explore the cultural meanings of nonhuman lives – animals, plants, and other organisms. What kind of meaning are we talking about—and what is the foundation of this meaning?

Ursula K. Heise: Rather than answering the question of the real value of animals and other nonhuman organisms, I wanted to explore the many ways we weave them into our stories and connect with them. I explore texts and artifacts that represent and explore not just the relationship between humans and nature, but also the ideological narratives about our own species. I purposefully talk about "meanings" in the plural, to emphasise that the meanings we grant animals and plants vary from culture to culture—and over time.

AD: The Norwegian deep ecologist Arne Naess promoted the intrinsic value of plants and animals, or biodiversity as such. Is this "intrinsic" value actually dependent on us?

UH: It is, because humans are the ones who attribute intrinsic value so something nonhuman. Naess' argument was that the value of nature lies not only in the instrumental functions it fulfills for humans. He resisted the old narrative where the purpose of nature is to provide humans food and resources.

So the old argument would be that biodiversity is useful for humans as well as useful for the ecosystems in which we live: Protecting biodiversity becomes important because ecosystems with more species tend to be more resilient and recuperate better after disasters or disruptions, so this is a solid scientific argument.

And then you have the argument that builds on the utility of single species. There are a myriad of medical resources and food resources among species that we have not even identified, deep in the rainforests of the Amazon. We have a self-interest in preserving such habitats. But it is interesting to note how fast this argument reaches its limit. Even the famous biologist E. O. Wilson, who has written several books on the future of nature and the conservation of biodiversity, admits—often in chapter 4 or 5 in his books—that this argument is only valid for a small number of species.

This is where Naess' argument, for all its limitations, still has some traction: on the basis of their utility for humans, we can argue only for the protection of a limited number of species. You are left with a score of species that no one cares about—and that it is difficult to imagine anyone would care about, even in the future, since they don't have any immediate value for humans.

AD: Is this because we do not know about them, or because we neglect them?

UH: Both, since most species are small and modest creatures. A few years ago, there was an enormous and costly project to build a database of all marine species—and in the process thousands of new ones were discovered. There is beautiful imagery online about the <u>census of marine life</u> that you can look up. It is almost like science fiction: many of the new organisms are unbelievably beautiful; others are so strange that they really look like species from other worlds. But these are all species that science knew nothing about until very recently. So they're not associated with any cultural or human meanings—not to mention stories or narratives. No indigenous peoples were interacting with them and there are no myths about them, simply because you need advanced deep-sea submarines to even see them. So, no human societies ever interacted with them and they are almost completely outside the human realm. What kind of argument would you enlist for their meaning, the meaning humans might give them? Anyone with the slightest critical sense will be prone to say: "We got along fine without them before we knew about them, so we will hardly miss them later. Why should we feel such an urge to preserve them?"

This is precisely what interests me: There should be reasons, perhaps with arguments like those of Arne Naess, that these and all other organisms have a right to exist. Or perhaps we should avoid the word "right," since this is a complicated philosophical and legal concept, and rather say that all species should have a claim on our ethics, some moral claim on humans—while at the same time not neglecting the moral claim that other humans have on us. Who gets to say what is to be done with the natural resources at hand in one particular place?

AD: Sometimes the interests of animals and human beings are directly opposed. One example you mention in *Imagining Extinction* is the relationship between humans and gorillas in the Congo, where local populations living in poverty are provoked by the enormous efforts of conservationist groups to save the gorillas, while their own pressing needs are neglected.

UH: On a more abstract level you could of course also argue that every dollar that is invested which doesn't have any obvious use for humans is money that could have gone to the poorest of the poor. On this level, the ethical priorities can be broken down to the allocation of resources.

How do we think about the claims of other humans and of nonhumans on our moral consideration? That is the question that some environmental justice advocates have grappled with, and that my own concept of "multispecies justice" seeks to capture.

AD: Whether we base ourselves on utilitarian principles or an ethics of rights and duties, we often end up with some sort of ethical accounting when we attribute values to species. With what value and importance does the deep-sea fish enter our considerations? Does it have an equal standard value, does it have an extremely low priority, or is it outside the list of priorities altogether? What mindset would we have to adopt in order to give other and distant species a reasonable consideration when we choose our priorities?

UH: On one hand, I draw on the multispecies-thinking that has emerged across different strands of research over the last few decades. In the last twenty years, we have begun taking seriously that human societies interact and coexist with a great number of other species. As Bruno Latour already argued in his actor-network-theory, this means that the division between human subjects and the objects of nature has been blurred. And what we usually consider human societies are in reality multispecies societies. It begins with our own bodies, which are colonies of different microorganisms that populate us, and which are a part of us to the extent that we couldn't even live without them. On the other hand, you have all the other species that we eat, and as such depend on—and then all the animals we keep as pets, which not only depend on us, but which we depend on in turn.

AD: There is the idea of symbiosis—and of sympoiesis—the co-construction and coevolution of life worlds, which Donna Haraway elaborates...

UH: Right. But the really tricky question is how to adjudicate colliding claims, plans, and demands between nonhumans and different groups of humans. Here the debate is just beginning, and the question of justice is extremely important. At the end of the process of writing *Imagining Extinction*, I felt a need to step away from the scientific discourse of biodiversity, which tends to be very abstract and often unhelpful. Science tries to say something universal about nature. But when it comes to legal concepts, the situation is different: Legal practices and ethics vary enormously from one place to another, from one culture to another. People love the idea of preserving dolphins and beautiful mammals, but they are less inclined to care about spiders and snakes and insects, which many people really dislike. There lots of instances where it is impossible to come to an agreement because of such preferences, and also because the notions of justice differ from culture to culture.

AD: So you have to start out with some sort of local validity?

UH: You must find out who is involved, who the stakeholders are. That is why Latour's idea of a "parliament of things" remains interesting. When we discuss the role of plants or animals, we give voice to the silent or voiceless—or at least allow them to become part of the conversation.

AD: This is also a little like Habermas's discourse ethics: we have to reconstruct what the involved parties, even unborn generations, would say. How would such an imagined political debate, involving the animals, take place and play out?

UH: We can take as an example the question of feral cats in cities, like here in Los Angeles. I respect and appreciate the idea that the cats can't be blamed for the environmental impact that results from their growing population. They have been abandoned by their owners, and now they are roaming the streets. It seems unreasonably cruel to simply say that they are a nuisance, that they kill too many birds, and that they need to be exterminated. The animal advocates and cat advocates say: "Hey—it's not the individual cat's fault that there are so many. People put them out there, they're just being cats." On the other hand, we must listen to the environmentalists, who emphasize that by letting the cats live, you indirectly sentence scores of other animals to death—enormous numbers of rodents, lizards, and birds. There is no innocent choice for us; we will simply not be able to honor everyone's claims. These are the situations that I am most interested in—where there is not an easy reconciliation, but where we need to accept that we have to make decisions about life and death. Inevitably, in that context, the question comes up who will make that decision. Here, I think Western environmentalists are often too hasty in saying something like, "we know what is in our human interest, or what is objectively, scientifically, the right thing to do." Postcolonial theorists and environmental justice advocates have been right in saying that this is illusory and that it's an overly universalistic global community you're postulating. Scientists are just one community—other groups of humans might have very different ideas about what we should do. So, for starters, we need to listen to these different stakeholders, and then also try to include the organisms on behalf of which these decisions are to be made.

AD: So even if the universal collective of humans, the "we" that is so hard to stop evoking, is misleading, there is still a sense in which there is a global collective to the extent that we are touched by the same situations. One could even argue that if a species is lost forever, it is humanity's loss. There is also another sense in which "we" are all touched by the same problems, such as climate change, which places us in a problem-community with other species. One could make the same argument about the interrelatedness of an ecosystem, where we are citizens of the same landscapes, so to speak. In your book you talk about eco-cosmopolitanism, but cosmopolitanism is already a fraught concept. What does an extended cosmopolitanism entail?

UH: You have to come up with ways of representing nonhuman species at a given location, and of doing it in a political sense. To find some way in which their interests can at least be heard. You have to establish some forum where these questions can be decided. As for animals, plants and other species, they would have to be given some sort of representation. That still involves science, but in a different way, since we need to draw on what we have learned about animal perception, about animal emotions and intelligence, and about how nonhuman species communities function. And that is where posthumanist theories of animal sentience come in—regarding the dissolving boundaries between the human and the nonhuman. The exceptionalism of humans is very questionable. Everything we thought was uniquely human, such as language, culture, tool usage, or knowledge of death, has turned out to be not uniquely human. Every time someone actually bothers to look for such characteristics, they turn out to exist in other species, too. Knowing about other animals, what their perceptual universe is, what their cultural universe is, is clearly crucial. Here I have to Frans de Waal in mind, who studies chimpanzee and bonobo cultures and politics – and you cannot really call it anything else without being grossly speciesist. What is really in the interest of another species? I think that is also where ecology and ethology really can help—to tell us something about the perceptual and experiential world of another species and hence its interests. But then of course that needs to be negotiated. How do you negotiate your interest in preserving a habitat for certain species versus the interests of communities to have better access to transportation or other conveniences which might destroy habitats? I think we need to begin to think of forums where both can be represented.

AD: Arne Naess's solution was to say that we have no right to reduce biodiversity or destroy habitats, except to satisfy our vital needs. The obvious problem, then, is defining vital needs—which Naess also tried to do. But ever since Plato wrote his *Republic*, it has been acknowledged that humans are not content with building a society of pure need, as Socrates suggests, where we eat a few vegetables a day and enjoy simple and healthy pleasures. Only some very rare tribes can be said to limit themselves to catering vital needs; and in the so-called civilized world, luxury and abundance is a rule, rather than an exception. So how are we to proceed?

UH: Maybe we can start from the opposite end and say that vital needs vary from one person to another, and from one community to another. It should be possible to begin without general rules or principles as to what human beings need, and rather ask: "Which of our activities and what forms of consumption are evidently superfluous and actually wasteful?" Some of us humans live in societies that are enormously inefficient and surround ourselves with a lot of things that do little or nothing to contribute to our quality of life. So maybe one way to start thinking about long-term sustainability would be to identify those things we clearly don't need. That's not going to get us all the way to sustainability, but it's an interesting first step for those of us who live in societies based on consumption. How much single-use plastics do we really need, for example, and what's the consequence of its use for other species?

AD: They have found out that it follows the hydrological cycle, so that thousands of tons of microplastics rain down on even remote areas where wild creatures live, exposing them to toxins. In addition, there are so-called invasive species, and a score of parasites that spread with human transportation routes, as we experience over and over whenever new parasites show up. In Norway, the government decided to exterminate a whole population of reindeer, because of a few cases of chronic waste disease. Here we are dealing with a choice that seemingly was made out of concern for the animals and to save future generations of reindeer, but which nonetheless led to mass slaughter.

UH: I guess you could argue that it is for the good of the coming generations, even if that is a speculative idea. In speculative fiction, there are writers who explore an even more extreme idea, like Orson Scott Card in his science fiction novel *Xenocide*. Set in a future world, on another planet that humans have colonized, there is a virus that may possibly be sentient—and the biodiversity of the planet depends on it—but it is actually lethal to humans. It is an interesting allegory of this problem you describe, when the lives of animals or other organisms are taken in the interest of future preservation. It's another case, like that of urban feral cats and songbirds, where no choice is completely non-violent.

AD: Especially to the extent that humans are colonizers of the planet in question. As Michel Serres has observed, it is all a question of who becomes the host and who becomes the guest who takes too much. We humans also behave in parasitical ways—infiltrating other species and habitats, taking without giving back, etc. Infiltration can perhaps be positive, as when they use genetic engineering to make the mosquitoes immune to the malaria they carry, but in the case of the reindeer in Norway, the chosen option was extermination. We would hardly accept the idea of killing people to avoid them becoming infected, right?!

[margin note: COULD THE REINDEER HAVE BECOME IMMUNE? (HERD IMMUNITY)]

UH: Right. Such a line of thought is taken straight out of the darkest chapters of eugenics, ideas that have been rightly condemned in the strongest terms. The other question, then, is to which degree and with what right we can extend that kind of philosophy to animal populations, and to future ones at that. To voice the interest of beings that are not yet born—be they humans or animals—is an exceedingly difficult task, and very complicated philosophically.

It's hard to anticipate what future people and future ecosystems will need.

AD: We also often end up with a conflict, which you point out in *Imagining Extinction*, between the environmentalists who tend to be more concerned about the whole and the ecosystem, and the animal rights activists who focus on the interests of the individual animals. Is a form of equity or justice based on biodiversity a common ground between them?

UH: I don't think multispecies justice is a way of reconciling the two: it's a way of highlighting the hard questions. Take the example of Australia, where there are more than twenty million feral cats. All these cats have become a serious threat to other animals and are pushing many endangered species toward full extinction. There was recently a program in Australia to systematically exterminate two million cats. So, we end up with eighteen million cats instead of twenty, but why are we so keen on getting rid of the cats when we know that there used to be marsupial lions in Australia who died out fifty thousand years ago? We're very concerned about Bengal tigers in India dying out, while we have a feral cat population that keeps growing. They may be the new predators. The question, then, is how we are to balance the arguments about biodiversity against individual animals. You can't just say that there is an automatic right for native species to exist in a particular place that non-native species can never attain.

AD: We end up with a conflict over territorial claims that we know all too well from human societies, for example the Israel-Palestine conflict. We often keep pointing out who was there first—without it being obvious that this is the only valid criterion. Is there no solution to the problem of coexistence?

UH: The striking thing after reading and comparing scientific and non-scientific literature on the problem of biodiversity is the realization that this is not really a scientific question. Science can inform us which species have so far existed in a biotope, how they are connected through food networks, and which effects different species have on each other. But it can't tell us which species combination should be there in the future. This is a normative choice based on values, and I think we deceive ourselves if we expect natural scientists to provide us with the answers. Yet, these are most often the authorities that conservationists rely on. I grant that science is extremely relevant and important, and I am not arguing against the importance of ecology as a science. But the question of which ecosystems Australia will have in the future is at this point ultimately a question of what human-altered ecosystem we want. Many younger biologists are beginning to recognize this.

AD: But where do we draw the line of what can be said to be natural and wild and what is domestic and created by humans? If the population of cats is out of control, is it not also by definition a wild species?

UH: That is definitely true; at a certain level they are beyond our control. I ran into this issue of unintended consequences in my own backyard in Los Angeles: there are neighborhood domestic cats who kill lots of birds, and I was inclined to think there were too many of them and that the owners needed to be encouraged to keep them indoors more. But we also have a population of rats in the yard, and I had no problem with that until I realized that they also eat the milkweed that I have planted to help monarch butterflies. Now I'm thinking that we should let in the cats, so that they can eat the rats, so that we can support the butterflies! So nature changes constantly, and the challenging task for environmentalists is finding a balance between conserving some parts of nature and letting other parts change. What seems certain is that we won't have a restoration of the old wilderness, but new kinds of wild instead.

AD: It is often highlighted that indigenous peoples don't have a concept of nature. Aborigines, for instance, have reportedly been invited to discuss the conservation of nature. But there is a barrier in the communication, since they can't fathom what this "nature" really signifies.

UH: Native Americans sometimes speak about nature as a house or a garden that needs to be tended for it not to deteriorate. This is very striking, because it is certainly not how white North Americans are tend to think of nature: as something that is best when it is disturbed as little as possible. We might need a different attitude, where we see nature as our home, something to be constantly cared for. What we need to ask, at least in an urban context, is what ecosystem with a high level of diversity we can aim for. What is an ecosystem that will be functional, both biologically and socially, in an urban context that includes millions of humans?

AD: To care, we also need to be aware of what we care for, of its presence. The number of insects is in dramatic decline, and most people don't care much about it. My father, who is an ornithologist, has noted that insect-eating migratory birds are also in steep decline, even in inland valleys in Norway. How do we translate such concerns into active care?

UH: It turns out that the source of the problem is not only insecticides, but also the monocultures—enormous fields with single crops like corn and wheat. In agroecology, which is concerned with sustainable and regenerative farming, it has been demonstrated that by planting trees and a greater variety of crops it is possible to create a greater biodiversity than even wild nature or pristine forests can sustain—and reduce or eliminate the need for pesticides. We need positive projects and positive stories like these.

AD: So the idea of the post-natural can maybe also become an attempt to transcend the melancholy inherent in much conservationism—where pristine nature and the wild are constantly deteriorating? Can we let go of these stories without ending up on the opposite extreme, where we see nature as some kind of machine that can be reprogrammed?

UH: I sometimes worry that the environmental literature I make my students read will paralyse them and make them depressed instead of inspiring them to action. What message are we giving them, ethically, when so much environmentalism ends up being about melancholy and apocalypse? Working on my book on extinct species, I read other books on the same topic for three to four years – something that made me very depressed at times! Most of this literature is about the negative human impact on nature and demands that we give up on things in a spirit of self-sacrifice. But there is rarely a positive vision of what we want. We need an encouraging and life-affirming message which says yes, there are actually ways of living in nature which makes it more beautiful and attractive, and which can help making it a better place to live also for other species. That is, I think, where the environmental justice movement and a movement for multispecies justice make a real difference.

AD: Where should we start?

UH: One interesting place to start are cities. We have hardly even begun the great and exciting task of making cities that are actively accommodating other species. Take a typical modern city made of glass and concrete. It may have a stylish design, but it is made with little concern for other species. Millions of birds collide with skyscrapers in Toronto and New York. Today, activists and ornithologists are working with the owners of these buildings to dress the windows in a film that is visible to birds, but not to humans. A German company is producing bricks with openings, allowing the birds to perch and build nests. They even have special bricks for different species, swallows and owls, for example. With these tools, we could build for humans and birds at the same time.

My favorite story is about the green-cheeked Amazon parrots in Los Angeles. The species is originally from Northeastern Mexico, and it is now endangered, mostly because of the illegal pet bird trade in the 1970s and 1980s, and also logging in the forests that were their habitat. Today there are some small but flourishing colonies of these birds in the United States, wild descendants of escaped pet birds. One of the colonies is in East Los Angeles, in Pasadena and the San Gabriel Valley. Since they are now a self-sustaining population, the California Bird Records

Commission added them to the offical list of California birds, making them "naturalized citizens," in a way. The Lab for Environmental Narrative Strategies at UCLA has made a short documentary about these birds called <u>Urban Ark Los Angeles</u>, as an inspiring way of thinking about the status of immigrant humans and nonhumans in our urban areas, and about multispecies justice more generally.

ENTERING A VASTER HISTORY

with Dipesh Chakrabarty

Dipesh Chakrabarty (b. 1948) is an Indian historian who currently teaches at the University of Chicago.

He is part of a second wave of postcolonial theorists, many of whom are inspired by Marx's ideas of class struggle but critical of the Marxist conception of history. In Chakrabarty's most famous work, *Provincializing Europe* (2008, 2000), he writes about how our notions of both past and future are characterized by grand narratives, constructed to make sense of history, while justifying entrenched hierarchies of dominance and power.

With the article, "The Climate of History: Four Theses," Chakrabarty helped popularize the concept of the Anthropocene within the humanities. Chakrabarty sees the Anthropocene as an integration crisis, where different perspectives need to be adapted to each other. If history previously facilitated ethnic and regional identities, he argues, we are now forced to create new frameworks against a background of natural history and hypercomplex ecological and economic networks.

In his latest book, *The Climate of History in a Planetary Age* (Chicago, Forthcoming), he revisits and expands his exploration of the significance of the climate crisis, as well as the distinction between the global and the planetary.

Anders Dunker: Your background is in postcolonial theory and you have written books and articles confronting the Western discipline of history with perspectives from India and other non-Western regions. At the same time, you are known as one of the first to write about climate science in connection with history. This unusual combination results in some very original thinking. How did the topic of climate first come up in your work?

Dipesh Chakrabarty: It began with a shock, a disaster, namely a series of forest fires in Australia in 2003 that destroyed a lot of beautiful natural places around Canberra. These were places that I had fallen in love with as a graduate student—every year, when I go back to Australia, I visit these places. In 2003, I brought an Indian friend to show him my favorite waterfall, called the Ginninderra Falls, and I was shocked to find that the whole park was burnt out.

Animals had been killed, there were burnt cars in front of the park—it looked like a scene from that movie *Mad Max*: completely dystopic. The region was going through a drought and the grass was completely yellow. So, it looked very dry, parched, and totally burned out. The big fire also destroyed about three hundred houses in Canberra and killed a few people and many, many animals. When I asked people what was going on, people said it wasn't a normal drought, it was climate change. I knew nothing about climate change—what I studied was rights and justice between humans, Thomas Hobbes, John Locke, Marx, Lenin, Gandhi, Mao, Gramsci, and other political thinkers. And I realized that my education as a historian hadn't given me the education I needed to understand all this, because this is something you can't understand without reading some natural science.

So, you start reading about the history of the planet and discover Earth System Science and about our relationship to the lithosphere, the biosphere, and the atmosphere. You know how critically we depend on the atmosphere to get the oxygen we need—and already here, the facts are staggering. The atmosphere has maintained its level of oxygen at an amazingly stable level. A little more and the forests would all burn. A little less and we would be suffocated. The balance has been kept for almost 400 million years. We are creatures of this atmosphere and we depend on it, but we had nothing to do with its creation or maintenance. And our industrial pollution affects this precarious balance. For me, insights like this placed humankind on a much bigger canvas. A canvas is actually a misleading image, since what we are realizing is that nature is precisely not a background, but rather is the foreground—there is no background!—and we are a part of it.

AD: These days, then, the scene itself is becoming the main character of the drama?

DC: Normally we treat nature as a landscape. There is a beach in the Basque country of Spain called Itzurun Beach. A Canadian photographer, named Edward Burtynsky, has a very interesting collection of pictures in a book on the Anthropocene. He has two photos of a couple on holiday sitting on that beach in front of some rocks. And the couple, they don't know that these rocks were critical for geologists for the discovery of evidence of the warming event that happened on this planet fifty-five million years ago, which is called the Paleocene-Eocene Thermal Maximum. These rocks were critical because they contained the evidence. But for the couple that is sunbathing, it is part of the beauty of the landscape. But when you read these stories, you realize that these rocks have a story to tell, which is relevant because the nearest example we have of global warming and its consequences is precisely here, in these rocks from more than fifty-five million years ago.

AD: That was about ten million years after the dinosaurs died out...

DC: Yes, and the temperature rose about 8 degrees Celsius, and there was devastation. But, back then, the temperature rose over a period of 10,000 years. Now, the temperature rises so much faster. So that is the nearest historical parallel, which has become disquietingly relevant. Given this knowledge, if I were to take a holiday in Itzurun now, I would not be able to help thinking about those rocks. This is a part of the shock of the Anthropocene. What used to be a stable landscape becomes a geological event in an unstable history.

AD: The Anthropocene signifies the epoch in which Earth's geophysical systems are affected and altered by humans. When this concept fully began catch on, so to speak, you had already written your article "The Climate of History: Four Theses." Maybe the article came out too early?

DC: When it was first published in India as an article in Bengali, hardly anyone read it. Then when it is was rewritten and published in English, it got a lot of attention.

AD: The first of your four theses about the climate of history states that, with anthropogenic climate change, the age-old distinction between natural history and human history collapses. What are the roots of that distinction? And what can the disciplines of natural history and human history learn from each other?

DC: It strikes me that the dialogue might be older than the division, so I think I exaggerated a bit when I said "age-old." It's really from the nineteenth century. If you look at Christian histories from before the nineteenth century, or even Comte de Buffon's history of creation from the eighteenth century, natural and human aren't separate, because God is the creator of both. Even if humans are special, they are not separate from nature. During the nineteenth century, the split between social sciences and natural investigations became sharper and you had the formation of new disciplines like anthropology and history. Then the division became consolidated and stronger. Historians and political thinkers tended to treat natural history as part of the givenness of the world.

If there was a mountain, it was something given, which didn't give rise to further questions. The mountain, the river, or the field just provided a setting for an historical event, like a battle. The surroundings could impose limitations on a battle, so if the river was not fordable in a certain season, then a battle would have to be postponed. Whether you look at agriculture, urban life, trade, or transport—it was all very dependent on seasons. Before modern times, roads were seasonal. Sailing ships would depend on trade winds, which blew at certain times of the year. So, in one way, natural history, along with nature itself, was seen as part of the givenness of human life, and part of that which constrained human action.

AD: So nature is, after all, a force in history, even for earlier historians?

CH: The historian Fernand Braudel was one of those who wanted to bring all that into view—the landscapes, the seasons—and he included them in his deep history, the longue durée. And yet, he still saw nature as fixed and cyclical. So, he saw these so-called natural factors as more dynamic than other historians, not just a static background, but something that actually had its own effects. But he didn't see them as ever drastically changing.

AD: Which is exactly what is happening with climate change. Nonetheless, in the past there would also be great upheavals in nature playing a role in human affairs: earthquakes, heat waves, storms, draughts, cold spells...

DC: At the same time when Braudel was writing there was the Oxford philosopher of history, Robin Collingwood. He was actually a kind of an intellectual disciple of Croce. He said that whereas nature can have events, it has no history. Nature has chronology—but only humans have motives and motivations. For this reason, he says, only humans have history. This is precisely why it is important to explain why someone did this or that when you write history—someone got angry, somebody felt insulted. He took it for granted that you can't write about a mad person's motivation—since the motivation has to be understandable to sustain and thus to explain an historical action. If we are writing about a peasant revolt, we are writing about a feeling, because the peasants are angry. They don't have bread, so we get a rebellion. They were angry because they felt they had been treated unjustly, and therefore they mobilized for battle.

AD: In a rationally motivated way, which is different from being mad with rage, I assume. A mad person is more like a natural phenomenon, like a volcano!

DC: Indeed, a mad person has become pure nature, a biological phenomenon. But the "normal" person has motivations. In the Indian *Subaltern Studies* that I was a part of in the 1980s, our most important guru, Ranajit Guha, argued, referring to the Italian philosopher and Marxist Antonio Gramsci, that it was wrong to compare peasant uprisings with volcanic eruptions and earthquakes, because they were not "natural" events. They were "historical": even in the most chaotic collective actions, such as wars and rebellions, there was consciousness and deliberation.

AD: So, what about climate change? The concept of the Anthropocene emphasizes that humans act like a force of nature, a force equal to the natural forces. What happens when humans go from being an historical agent to a force of natural history. Does it mean that we act like a mad person—that we don't know what we are doing? That, even if we can observe the process that we are part of, it seems to us as mindless and unstoppable as a volcano?

DC: When I read about climate change, I was shocked to see scientists declare that, with our industrial capacity to produce climate gases, humans have impacted the cycle of ice ages and interglacial periods, a rhythm otherwise determined by variations in the earth's orbit and the axis of the planet. From what I had previously understood, you could obviously change nature and affect local weather by planting trees and destroying forests. But this claim was something different—because human beings can affect the climate of the planet as a whole. And our effect is equal to that of enormous volcanos or an asteroid strike. That scientists could describe humanity's impact in such terms was overwhelming—yet at the same time I had a clear idea that nobody has wanted or chosen to create such effects.

AD: Still, the consequences are a result of human choices. Some argue against the description of the Anthropocene as a shock or a sudden realization of all our unintended effects on the planet. The French historians Cristophe Bonneuil and Jean-Baptiste Fressoz argue that climate change is just one of many damaging results of modernization, and that it is an act of self-deception to say that we didn't know about it, since, historically, there have been so many warnings about pollution and the over-exploitation of nature. What do you think about this line of argument?

DC: Their provocative stance is that we have entered the Anthropocene with open eyes, or that we have chosen to close our eyes. I don't think this is fully convincing, since climate change is the most central factor of the Anthropocene, and since it really is a quite recent topic—even if thirty years have passed since NASA scientist James Hansen presented the dangers of climate change to the American Congress in 1987. Postcolonial criticism, which has been my own field, began at roughly the same time, but without any awareness of climate change or global warming. Aside from a few experts and specially interested people, it took a long time for the problem to take hold. When I started writing about global warming around the year 2000, I was one of the first in the humanities to put climate change on the agenda.

AD: So, the question is whether we should see climate change as a separate problem or as phenomenon that is an integral part of other human-made environmental problems. Modernity has come with an abandonment of inhibition—a process of disinhibition, Fressoz says. People have had their qualms about overfishing. They have been concerned with the felling of forests, with pollution. People have argued that nature doesn't get a chance to recover and regenerate, that it is brought out of balance. Every time such arguments arise, the rhetoric has, according to Fressoz, been the same: modernization comes at a price worth paying because society will be fundamentally improved!

DC: What they don't account for when they criticize the rhetoric of modernity is that unless you see it as a conspiracy, you must relate to the fact that millions and millions of people have also desired modernization, in spite of some very eminent critics. India is a very good case because India produced a man like Gandhi—and Gandhi was decidedly against industrialization.

AD: How did he argue against it?

DC: He was against big cities. He said that big cities brutalized people. He said industrial civilization makes you greedy and causes disease—because most diseases, he argued, stem from greed: we overeat, we overconsume, so we get problems. But even then, before he was killed, Indian politicians sidelined him as a very respected figure who was nevertheless not to be listened to or followed. The argument was this: given our growing numbers, there was no option, they said, other than those of artificial fertilizers, industrial production, and large-scale farming and production, because otherwise you could not feed all these people. If you followed Gandhi, they thought, the population would collapse.

AD: An argument which might be disputable but seems convincing to most people. Isn't it also because people desire a certain material standard?

DC: People in India have voted for a party with fascist traits. Not because they are fascists, but because it is widely considered as the party that will bring the most economic growth and create more work; the party that will transform India and make this densely populated country look like America.

We must remember that our technical, industrial civilization has also made it possible for us to increase the number of people on the planet and to help them live longer. Life expectancy has risen, even among the poor, who may not have the best lives, but who now live longer. We would not have been able to accomplish this without cheap and plentiful energy. And the source for that was fossil fuels.

People's desire for a higher living standard is neither a product of a conspiracy nor something planned. Therefore, I am inclined to think that people who only produce a critique of capitalism don't give us a way to think deeply about the desire for these things.

AD: Can't we also see modernization as driven by competition as much as desire, as a mass mobilization or a race that knows no limits?

DC: It is difficult to distinguish between competition and imitation. If you look back on five hundred years of European expansion, other nations saw Europeans improving their standards by taking from each other and by expanding, by colonizing. We tend to learn from others. Japan is a good case in point. Why did the Japanese translate so many European texts and go for industrialization without being forced to do so? Because Europeans set up a game, which came to appear like it was the only game in town. So, all those outside Europe's empires who objected to it were seen as minor voices. And I don't think anyone would deny the existence of these minor voices. And it was not the case that these minor voices were suppressed. We read them like poets, like we read the Romantic poets lamenting industrialization. Modernization has extended our lifespans and appears to have made our lives more secure. The rhetorical question is this: do you really value individual human lives? Or would you prefer for the population to collapse?

AD: Proponents of limiting growth are criticized and labeled Malthusians by those who still favor it. At his most extreme, Malthus professed closing hospitals and building cities in malaria-infested swamps in order to ensure sufficient death-rates to compensate for rising birthrates.

DC: If you support the idea of limiting the human population by other than democratic means, who will then suffer? The poor. The rich will always find a way.

AD: So Western critics of capitalism and growth fail to take the situation of the poor seriously enough?

DC: What I say is that such critics don't help us to think through the most fundamental desires of human beings—the deep longing to improve their circumstances—unless of course you think of all such desires as something fabricated as a result of some kind of a conspiracy or ideological assault produced by capitalism.

I think this psychology which draws us toward modernization and material prosperity reflects some of the short-term attitudes people have. I wrote an essay on the planetary climate crisis and its relationship to air conditioners in Indian cities. The thing is that all Indian cities are becoming heat islands. They are getting hotter and hotter as more and more high-rises go up, and they are made of concrete which emits a lot of heat. So, air-conditioner sales are booming in India.

AD: In Paul Hawken's book *Drawdown*, he lists the eighty most important things we can do to slow down or even reverse the greenhouse effect. Improved air conditioning turns out to be number one! How does India relate to such efforts?

DC: Here lies the problem. In 2017, there was an international summit in Kigali, Rwanda, to phase out old fashioned air conditioners, which are very bad for the environment. India bargained hard to be classified among the countries that would be the slowest to make the transition. This is because air conditioners are totally tied up with people's ambitions. Air-conditioner sales are booming from people buying air conditioners for the first time in their lives. It is their first unit. And they are doing it in the slums—very poor people. When people are asked why you bought it, their answers are telling: "It is the first time I had a proper sleep. I have a sense of well-being that I've never had because we are six people sleeping in the same room. It is the first time, some say, that my son can sit up all night and prepare for his entrance exams to medical school without being eaten up by mosquitoes." As a human being and a parent, you think about your child's advancement, and the air conditioner fits into the time-horizon of that expectation. It's that simple. They don't relate to what will happen to the city in twenty years' time or to the Earth in a hundred years. The more environmentally friendly air conditioners are expensive and complicated to install. They are out of reach for most people in the slums and for the middle class, too. And the medical exams are tomorrow.

If you don't engage with the problem of the environment at that level of human existence, you don't really understand it. What I say is that when you go down to this level, you also engage with humans as decision-making agents and get an understanding of our decision templates. Our focus on immediately relevant concerns has probably helped us to survive in the past. There is a kind of focus on the immediate, a kind of inherent short-termism. It is probably an evolved trait.

AD: So we sacrifice what seems distant in time and space for what is closer at hand. Given this self-interest, is it unavoidable then that future generations and other species will always be a low priority?

DC: It is not necessarily self-interest either. If your friend or relative has cancer, you want the best treatment thinkable, it is a higher priority than anything else.

AD: So can this personal and political psychology work in a situation where there is also a pressing need to handle climate change, environmental degradation, and the sixth extinction?

DC: Personally, I believe that these are evolved habits, because they are based on rewards. The circuit between action, effect, and consequence is short and easy to grasp.

Some of the planetary phenomena that we affect, on the other hand, are operating within very large time spans. We become part of slow and enormous processes that force us to think on an altogether different timescale than we are used to. The positive consequences of allowing oneself a little more pollution, to fell a forest or to consume the groundwater, are immediate. But the negative consequences for the environment only manifest themselves as a total effect—often further afield in time. For instance, the hydrological cycle has a double cycle. Even if rain and evaporation are fast, it can take thousands of years before aquifers are replenished and tens of thousands of years for melted glaciers to reform. Even if you cut down on oil emissions now, it will still take a few hundred years to get back to something closer to normal levels. David Archer has written about what he calls "the long thaw" and argues that with our emissions we have already called off the next ice age by maybe fifty thousand years. The longest perspectives have to do with biodiversity. If we completely ruin the diversity of species, it will take millions of years for it to come back. The problem of biodiversity should be treated with the same seriousness as we treat the problem of fossil fuels.

AD: You have stated that humankind operates as a geophysical force, yet we don't necessarily have the power to counteract the damage that we do. Are we, in other words, subject to natural limitations that we just cannot negotiate?

DC: Here we are dealing with another big question that I am grappling with, that of limits. If you look at European thinkers of the seventeenth century—Locke, and even before him Grotius writing the laws of the sea—you'll find that the seventeenth century thinkers had visions of abundance. Plenty of land, plenty of food: the oceans are brimming with food for human consumption. And the religious idea is also important, i.e., that God has provisioned the earth for us. Also, in the eighteenth century, for instance in Kant's writings, there is a vision of plenty. There is enough for everyone, so we don't really need to fight. We fight because God has not made it easy for us to become reasonable. He wants us to discover reason on our own, through strife and conflict. So we are erroneous creatures. We make mistakes, and our mistakes take the form of oppression, inequality, and wars. But through all that, God wants us to become reasonable.

AD: So we gradually correct ourselves through a kind of collective learning process. Shouldn't that also entail getting to know our own limitations and the limitations of the world?

DC: Only from the nineteenth century onward do we encounter a real doctrine of scarcity. In economics, we say that the price of the commodity must reflect its scarcity. The argument resurfaces in the 1972 report of the Club of Rome called "The Limits to Growth." If we look at climate change, we find a reprise of the same argument. The fundamental thought is that the world is one, it has one atmosphere, the oceans are interconnected, and this one world leads us to the idea of a world with limits. It cannot be endlessly exploited.

Some have objected that climate change advocates in fact promote what amounts to an injustice in the name of "one world." An early argument of this kind, by

Indian environmentalist activists Sunita Narain and Anil Agarwal, developed the notion of measuring emissions on a per capita basis. They said basically you have no right to equate emissions in the West with emissions in India. And so they argued against what they saw as a one-world-ism, which for them was basically hogwash.

AD: So the argument is that it is unjust for rich, industrialized nations to force limits upon countries like India that have historically emitted far less.

DC: They would say you have already emitted so much per capita compared to us that we should now be allowed to pollute in order to industrialize. A lot of discussion about climate change, especially in the Global South, has been about that. The problem is that the thresholds of global warming and higher temperatures are valid, even if it is unjust that the Global South will have to limit themselves.

AD: So these negotiations are based on justice, whereas the limitations of nature are absolute. You are very concerned with this contradiction. But what is the main problem here?

DC: There is a text by Immanuel Kant where he says that humankind can acquire reason through history on four conditions—and one of them is that we have unlimited time! The classic vision of abundance is also a vision of abundant time, an open future for humankind. At the end of World War I, we set up the United Nations on the assumption that any problem that was a global problem could be dealt with by this body of nations following the same Kantian presupposition that the amount of time we have to solve our problems is unlimited. Every calendar was an open calendar. Think about peace between Israelis and Palestinians. It's an open calendar. The Israelis, for example, might have it in mind to work for five hundred years to consolidate their state. Our governing institutions don't work as well when we are given a finite and closed calendar with absolute deadlines.

AD: And this kind of deadline is almost unprecedented in world history.

DC: Unique. And climate scientists emphasize that we have to act quickly.

AD: Despite hesitation, and great difficulty, in mobilizing to solve these problems, at least the IPCC has been uncompromising in saying that we only have ten years to turn things around. Doesn't it help to be given clear imperatives?

DC: The IPCC is a child of the UN, and there is a contradiction here because the climate crisis can be defined as a one-world problem. The panel is trying to give us a plan of action that applies to the whole world when the fact is that we are negotiating and adjusting the proposed limit to 2.0 degrees Celsius. This has much less to do with tipping points in nature than with political interests. It is a politically negotiated limit. If we had a world government, these questions wouldn't be open to negotiation. We would have a one-world government dealing with one-world problems. But the structure we have to rule the world with is such that all problems of a global nature must go through the UN, where different countries have a right to negotiate and argue.

AD: So limits that are dictated by the limits of time, resources, and nature are absolute, and yet we keep expecting growth?

DC: The German historian Reinhard Koselleck defined what he called the *neuzeit*, the new times, and understood it to be a time where the distance between the horizon of experience and the horizon of expectation is getting bigger. As you start believing in technology's capacity to change the world, you also come to believe in a future that may have wonders you can't imagine. Your imagination of the future is no longer based on just your experience because you know that the future could be completely different from the world of your grandfather. You think that your grandfather would be totally surprised by your present, just as the world of your grandchild would be completely different. The problem with climate change is that the future has collapsed right into our present. So the Koselleckian definition of our times has changed—the two horizons have in a way started overlapping.

AD: But still, we try to buy ourselves an escape through a technological leap. We are a little like gamblers who think we don't have to economize, because anytime soon, we could win big.

CH: So the gambling habit is still there. The Paris Agreement assumes that in order to stay below 2 degrees, there will be technology by 2070 or 2080 that makes our emissions negative. So not just zero, but negative. They think we will be able to scrub the air of carbon and sequester it somewhere.

AD: Which, in the worst-case scenario, is basically an illusion or simple rhetoric?

DC: Exactly—at least for now. Those who wrote the Paris Agreement are still living in Koselleck's time, in a modern time. But those who have a more dystopic vision think that that time has already collapsed.

Most politicians, in keeping with the UN vision of unlimited time, say we can solve the problem. Scientists, on the other hand, say that if we don't do something now, we are facing a disaster in the future.

AD: So the question is whether we should extend a culture of technological optimism or instead adopt a realist-pessimist perspective and prepare ourselves for absolute limits.

DC: We must realize that our expectations are defined by our cultural background. We live in a culture where we expect technology to solve all of our problems, since technology already has helped us overcome so many challenges. Based on our own experience, we believe in this technological magic, this redemption. At the same time, if climate scientists are right—which we have no reason to doubt—the coming crisis will also change our experience and expectations. We make new narratives and try to adjust to new historical roles. One of them is that we are now the biggest earth movers.

AD: You mean in a physical sense, by the erosion we create?

DC: Yes, all the physical processes in which soil is moved. For instance, we humans move much more earth around than the natural system does. Our yellow machines—the caterpillars—that move earth kind of symbolize this. I grew up with women, mostly very poor, moving earth in baskets carried on their heads when buildings were being constructed. But now, caterpillars are everywhere. And you can buy models of these machines for your children—and they grow up thinking that this is normal. They become earth movers. For these children, we have somehow normalized our capacity for earth moving. But this game also helps children acquire Anthropocenic agency. They partake symbolically in geomorphology. This is the way children perceive it, as something we enjoy, a game.

AD: Some people talk about our capacity to change the planet as something good, even going so far as talking about a "good Anthropocene." What do you make of embracing our role as earth movers and weather changers?

DC: The notion of the good Anthropocene comes from the idea that if we have transformed the earth into a spaceship, anyway, let's develop our technological instruments and do it well. I think that works well if we are talking about airplanes, which *we* have designed, not to mention piloted, maintained, and repaired. But I don't think we fully know how the earth system is designed. So, it is one thing to take charge of something that you have designed, and to make improvements to that design. It is quite another to try to take charge of something which you haven't designed and whose design you don't even fully understand.

AD: So rather than being like steering a ship, it is like riding a horse. You risk being thrown off if you don't know how the horse moves.

DC: That is a very good analogy, in fact. Still, many people remain dedicated to the idea of the good Anthropocene and "spaceship Earth." The ship metaphor also figures in the writings of Carl Schmitt in his writings about power and space. He claimed that when Europeans built vessels that could sail on the open sea, a new mode of dwelling appeared in which people were wholly dependent on technology. If the ship didn't work, you died. This is something we all practice when we fly. We submit ourselves to technology for a couple of hours. Peter Haff says that humanity as a whole now uses technology in this way, that we submit ourselves to technological systems. We depend on the "technosphere," the manmade infrastructure surrounding the earth. He makes a calculation that if we take away our current technologies, the human population will drop to a few million. We have made the civilized world into a kind of ship where the lives of seven billion passengers depend on the ship's functions.

AD: The problem, however, is that our technological innovations are now destroying the ship. Peter Sloterdijk has compared it with Phileas Fogg, who, in *Around the World in 80 Days*, starts burning the ship to keep the engine going. Rather than burning the ship, we have to learn to rebuild it, even while we are out on the open seas...

DC: Such ideas can easily lend themselves to arguments about geoengineering. Some people strongly support these arguments, like David Keith at Harvard, who wrote a book called *A Case for Geoengineering*. He has been funded by Bill Gates, and he discloses that upfront in the book in a gesture of saying—"I declare myself interested." And his argument is that we have already changed the planet and the atmosphere so much that geoengineering is only an extension of this trend of making the planet work better for us. I read the work of a geologist who claims that if you did that for 50 or 100 years, the sky would turn permanently white, not blue.

AD: This imparts a very disquieting sense of living in a post-natural world, in a time after nature. Others predict that vegetation would suffer and that ecosystems and agriculture would be affected. There might be some beneficial effects, but also a lot of negative effects, and they would be distributed unevenly across regions and populations. How can it be that it now seems more feasible to adjust the world to ourselves than to adjust ourselves to the world?

DC: One thought is that we have reached a point of no return and we can do no more than nostalgically consider how we should have acted. I once heard a geologist say that we have lost the reverence we should have had for the earth. Meaning that we should have been much less interventionist and should have treated the planet with much greater respect and care.

AD: Now that we are seeing nature being threatened, don't you think that such a reverence could return, or grow stronger than ever, with a new kind of *stimmung*, or mood, as Heidegger calls it. Aren't we beginning to see how precious the plant and animal kingdoms are, and beginning to change our culture accordingly?

DC: I think this sentiment could grow. But at this moment, we have not yet struck that mood. The previous US elections indicated that climate is not a concern. The same happens in other countries. In India, many people perceive the climate as a distant crisis. Like China, India is focusing on the international power game. The middle class are getting enthusiastic about the prospect of a strong India. What secures reelection is military prowess and the chance to get a seat at the big table—the security council. The Indian middle class has just come into the pleasures of consumption. And they are consuming like there is no tomorrow. A friend of mine even said, "Now it's our turn." On a human level it makes complete sense. At the same time, there is massive environmental damage. I read in a newspaper that thirty-one hills have disappeared in Rajasthan—they were illegally leveled to the ground to be used for construction materials. When China had a huge demand for metal ore during the preparation for the Olympics, the number of illegal mines in India were figured in the tens of thousands. And that was just the illegal mines. There is also a great displacement of wild animals. Some years ago, the deputy mayor of Delhi was killed by monkeys...

AD: How?

DC: They had gotten into his kitchen, and, when he tried to chase them out, they pushed him over the rail of his balcony. In other places, leopards are moving into the cities, often killing domestic dogs—an easy prey. Some tigers teach their cubs to kill humans. Such conflicts are an ongoing problem connected to the Anthropocene. When nature changes, animals and plants move. Microbes and small animals with short life spans can evolve more quickly, and birds can migrate to other territories, but larger animals have greater difficulties.

AD: And we humans face the same challenge—how to adapt to a changing and more unstable environment.

DC: As the problems grow, we will respond and adapt, but not without great difficulty and resistance. It is not like people will sit down around a table and say, "OK, so from tomorrow onwards..." That's not how history happens. Experience will goad us away from being indifferent. We will have to become different people. I think the challenge is to think in a more complex manner and more long-term, but people prefer to live with what Jane Bennett and Latour would call "thin descriptions," which are, in essence, extreme simplifications.

We want to live in a world consisting of my life, my body, my loved ones, and my house. Many things are left out. When the sun shines, we say it is a nice day and don't account for the climate. Capitalism thrives because of such thin descriptions. When you make something into a commodity, you simplify it. When you buy a plot of land, it is just a rectangle on a map—and even if you are told how many trees there are, the contract says nothing about the insects, the earthworms.

AD: But do we not also find ourselves in a situation wherein the landscapes, and the stories they are part of, get more complicated—where, so to speak, the plot thickens?

DC: Our simplifications no longer function. And this is also what I meant by the collapse of the barrier between human history and natural history. This distance from nature cannot be sustained. Yet, that hardly means anyone will stop simplifying the world.

AD: In your article "Anthropocene Time," you speak about the philosopher Husserl and how, in a famous passage, he insists that the earth doesn't move. It is a fact that it moves astronomically, but in experience it stands still.

DC: Phenomenologically the earth does not move. Our experience is a simplification. Even for the astronomer who walks to the observatory, the earth doesn't move. Existentially, the scientist stands on solid ground. But maybe that is changing, too, if we are really headed for a period with more earthquakes, more tsunamis, more volcanic activity because of climate change, as some geophysicists predict. The earth will move more, and our simplifications will be challenged more often and lose the support of experience.

AD: So we have the problem that, although we need to think in more complex terms, society encourages us to simplify?

DC: Absolutely. The commodity that Marx thinks with is created by acts of purification or simplification. Bruno Latour gives a very good example. When you bought milk from the milkman in the old days, he would bring a cow to your doorstep—something I have experienced myself. And you always had to boil the milk, because there could be bacteria in it. These days you must pasteurize it and remove the bacteria. So, for the milk to become a commodity, you need to simplify it. Similarly, in mining, when you look for iron, you don't necessarily find pure iron ore. You find iron mixed with other metals and minerals. You find a compound and your factory then has to purify it. What Latour calls "purification," which Jane Bennett calls "simplification," is a large part of capitalism, and the simplification of nature is what has allowed us to capitalize on it.

AD: But this simplification also means that many things are hidden from our sight: the residue from mining, the exploitation of workers and nature, the constricted and painful life of the dairy cow, factory farms and slaughterhouses, the clearing of rainforests for plantations and grazing. Given that we live in cities and have a distant and abstract relationship to nature, it is perhaps no wonder that we can't internalize these facts or experience them directly.

DC: Existentially, we tend toward simplification. Capitalism brings an additional level of simplification. The ironic thing is that modern civilization's simplification of nature, on a technological and capitalist level, also helps us discover all the complex relationships that we tend to overlook. It is no coincidence that Latour's background is in Science Studies.

AD: So, science grasps the complexity of the world . . .

DC: But it also gives us simplified technological products—a lifestyle that is increasingly based on distance from nature. All this worked well until science started telling us that industrial society causes complex problems, precisely because of the way we have simplified and purified nature in our production processes.

AD: It seems that the challenge is to reconcile our own simple lives—which often seem complicated enough—with hyper-complicated industrial society and gigantic planetary systems. How can we exist on both levels?

DC: In one of my latest texts, I emphasize that scientists are also private persons. When they look at the implications of what they have discovered, they experience very human emotions. They feel hope, or they feel desperation or anguish. In this way, they bring geo-history into the picture and they act more like humanists. They reconfigure facts, create narratives, and tell stories that make sense, that create optimism or pessimism. For this reason, I also read them as historians.

AD: Where are your own feelings, here? How drastic do you think climate change will become? Like other people who read extensively about the matter, I assume that you negotiate with yourself and try to process, on a personal level, what seem to be realistic predictions.

DC: Most people my age, who are about to retire, go to financial advisers who all assume a rate of return on your savings with calculations that do not yet take into account the effects of climate change. So, you retire thinking that it will be business as usual. Everyone tacitly imagines that the world we know will last at least until they are gone. I know that oil, coal, and gas companies hire economists to analyze scenarios. Because they are also asking: Will we be in business in twenty years, or whatever? Yet, in public statements, you won't find a CEO of one of these big companies telling us that society, the market, or their business will collapse. So, I don't have a clear answer to your question, apart from the fact that denial is, in various ways, a part in our lives—which leads us back to the bigger question.

AD: If our lifestyle proves unsupportable, how can we escape denial—give it up, at least in part? How do we deal with our attachments and habits?

DC: If you ask me personally, for instance, "Would I be willing to be much poorer than I'm used to being?" Then I think of my childhood in Calcutta, which was much poorer, but I was happy. So maybe there are resources there, mental resources, resources of habit—simple things. For instance, the amount of water I consume, showers and everything, is simply not available in Calcutta the way I live when I go back and stay with relatives. So I make do with less water, because everybody does.

AD: So the West, in other words, has much to learn from the rest of the world? Can we imagine a reversal of the geographical pattern of imitation, like what Vandana Shiva proposes—where the Western world can learn from Indian smallholders—from societies that are less dependent on modern technology?

DC: Paradoxically, poor countries may find themselves at an advantage. Poorer people are less attached to capitalist networks than people in richer countries. Asking peasant smallholders to give up some modern habits is not too difficult, since they are less involved in systems of capitalism. But the question of whether their politicians will take this road is another matter.

ON CRISIS, COLLAPSE, AND TIKOPIANS

with Jared Diamond

Jared Diamond (b. 1937) is an American historian, geographer, and anthropologist.

In *The Third Chimpanzee: Human Evolution and Prominence* (1991), Diamond examines our close kinship with higher-ranking monkeys and how small genetic variations can make a huge difference. Man's dominion over Earth and our destructive inclinations are an important subtopic pointing to subsequent books. In Diamond's best-known work, *Guns, Germs and Steel* (1997), he uses a global long-term perspective and examines the human relationship to the environment as one of the most important keys to understanding which peoples and cultures came to characterize and dominate the world, and who succeeded in competition with other cultures.

In Diamond's models, random and particular geographical conditions work together with universal principles of cultural growth, communication, and proliferation. The interaction between the environment and culture is also the theme of his later book *Collapse* (2005). In *The World Before Yesterday* (2012), Diamond discusses what the modern world can learn from traditional societies, starting with hunter-gatherer communities. The crisis as a phenomenon and challenge is the theme of Diamond's latest book, *Upheaval: Turning Points for Nations in Crisis* (2019).

Anders Dunker: In our time we can't talk about the future without considering the fact that we live in a moment of great crisis. Your latest book combines personal crisis with political ones. What inspired your project?

Jared Diamond: Both the global crisis and the crisis I perceive in the American political system. The political crises that I look at are taken from the recent history of countries that I know well, counties where I have lived; and, with one exception, they are countries where I speak the language: Finland, Indonesia, Chile, Germany, and Australia. The exception is the study of the crisis in Japan in the Meiji era. I don't speak Japanese, although my wife Marie has Japanese relatives, and she has also contributed directly to the perspectives in my book. She is a clinical psychologist and one of her specialties is helping people through personal crisis: relationship breakdowns, the death of a loved one, financial crisis, job crisis, health problems. All these crises send the same signal: they make you realize that the way that you're approaching life just doesn't work. As a first step one tends to overgeneralize, thinking "everything in my life is messed up." So the first challenge for the therapist is making the patient understand: "Your husband or wife walked out on you—so yes you have a relationship problem—but the rest of your life works ok." The solution is to do what's called "drawing a fence" to separate what needs to be changed from what is OK.

And then there are the predictors of crisis outcome, because for a therapist dealing with a crisis, there is always the danger that the patient may relapse to the old state, and the worst that can happen is suicide. This is not only devastating to them, but also to the therapist—what worse rejection could there be than that you couldn't save them? So crisis therapists meet each week to discuss who is dealing with their crisis and who not. They look at the outcome predictors, and the outcome predictors—many of them are what you would think: Are you getting any help from friends? Are there models of others who have dealt with similar crises? Have you dealt with big crises before or is this your first life crisis, ego strength comes in, self-confidence—things like that? As we talked about these outcome predictors, I realized that the same crisis predictors apply to national crisis.

I study each country, looking at the outcome of that country's crisis from the perspective of these dozen outcome predictors. For example: Japan in the Meiji era got lots of help from the U.S., France, Britain, Germany. Finland, when it was attacked by the Soviet Union, got no help—none of its allies helped. Sweden permitted some volunteers, but the Swedish government offered minimal help. So that's just an example of an outcome predictor that differs.

AD: The title of one of your former books was *Collapse: How Societies Choose to Fail or Succeed*. How to differentiate between crisis and collapse? What does a collapse mean on a political or national scale?

JD: A collapse can be seen as a failed response to a crisis. In fact, in the countries that I've looked at, none of them have collapsed in response to the particular crisis they were in—but of course for modern Germany and modern Japan, the crisis was the collapse of 1945. Germany has responded reasonably successfully to the disaster of 1945; Japan still has problems but is getting on. The countries that I write about in my book and where I have lived happen to be ones that have not suffered full collapses. I haven't lived in Afghanistan or in Somalia, but if I had, then I would have had to ask myself what the nature of those collapses is.

AD: But in *Collapse*, you talked about a series of societies that sort of collapsed for good—in the sense that something irreversible happened. Do you see such a threshold approaching in any of the current crises?

JD: Yes, of course. On a very big scale. The United States has big problems today, but we are in a relatively early stage. So a collapse is not imminent in any way. But across the world: come back thirty years from now—well, I won't be around—but there is a real chance that First World societies will have collapsed.

AD: So a crisis is a chance to learn—and you can learn from the crises of others or from history—but if we are in an unprecedented crisis, we somehow have to learn from the future and from predictions. Does that make the world crisis entirely different? Do we have to learn from predictions of the future rather than from mistakes of the past?

JD: You can learn from your own crisis, in fact. In the first chapter of my book, I mention that the Chinese sign for "crisis" consists of two written characters. One signifies danger, the other opportunity. So a crisis is a danger and also an opportunity. Winston Churchill had an expression: "Never let a good crisis go to waste." You can learn something form a crisis—you *may* be able to learn something, but not every country does.

AD: In the TV series *Closer to Truth* some years ago, the host, Robert Kuhn, asked you about the destiny of mankind from a cosmic perspective: what our future might hold in a thousand, ten thousand, a hundred thousand years. Your answer was that the next fifty years are the only thing that matters. Now you talk about the next thirty years.

JD: Of course! Who cares about a thousand years from now? The only thing to care about is getting through the next thirty years. If we get through the next thirty years, then the chances of a bright future are good. When my wife and I decided to have kids we really discussed whether it was worthwhile, but now one of my two sons has already said he is doubtful if he wants to have children, because he doesn't like the prospects of the state of the world. This has become a fairly common answer in the United States today. People say they don't want to have children because they don't like the prospects.

AD: Culturally, that is a drastic effect of the crisis. But on the other hand, you get the impression that most people tacitly assume that everything will continue as normal, that things will sort themselves out. Do we feel too safe, too confident?

JD: Yes, indeed. The British author and lexicographer Samuel Johnson, as described in the biography by James Boswell, has a sentence: "Believe me, Sir, if a man knows that he is going to be hanged in a fortnight, it wonderfully concentrates the mind." Similarly, for us, if there is a not an imminent crisis, then we tend to think that things will be OK. It usually takes a big jolt to make people adopt major change. Yet there are cases, there are hopeful cases, of countries that have adopted change without waiting for disaster—and the prime example in Europe is the foundation of the EU, and its predecessors in the fifties: the European Coal Community and then the Steel Community and the Common Market, which were launched by Konrad Adenhauer and other European leaders of the 1950s because they didn't want to wait for a World War III. They were acting in anticipation of the crisis—but you could also see it differently and say they already had the crisis of World War II.

AD: The opposite effect of such learning and concentration, it seems, is denial. Yet I recall a striking story in *Collapse* where you describe people reacting very differently to the danger of a dam bursting, depending on how close to the dam they live.

JD: Yes: they become more and more concerned the closer they live to the dam, until you reach those who live right under the dam—and they are not scared at all. They are in denial. Where we are sitting now, there is a dam exactly 1.1 miles up the street, and Marie and I live perfectly happy here. We don't think about the dam, although visitors occasionally ask us.

AD: So the tendency toward denial competes directly with the impulse to act on imminent danger?!

JD: Yes. Denial to a certain extent is healthy. Marie and I decided to live in this house. One can argue about whether that decision was right, but—having made that decision—we don't think about the dam. One could say that the best thing would be to buy a house somewhere else. The next best thing would be to buy the house and to deny the problem of the dam. The worst decision would be to buy the house and worry day and night.

AD: So denial is the second worst out of the three?

JD: Exactly!

AD: So our situation is created by our own decisions—decisions we could make or not make. In *Collapse* you list different factors that determine a society's survival, and the last two are knowledge about our circumstances and our ability to act upon that knowledge. To begin with the first one: Do you see lack of knowledge and understanding as a major impediment? Do we know enough, so that it all depends on our capacity to act on what we know?

JD: Some of us know enough . . . And when we say, "our situation" here in the U.S., there are problems in the United States that I am blind to. There are also problems of the U.S. and of the world that I am familiar with, such as the problem of climate change. Thirty years ago, very few Americans took climate change seriously. Thirty years ago, even most climate scientists were not convinced that the climate was getting warmer because there are fluctuations from year to year. If each year was mathematically 0.1 degree warmer than the previous year, after fifteen consecutive years of 0.1 degree ramped up, there wouldn't be any doubt. But it's not that way: there are fluctuations from year to year. So the first question was whether the climate was really getting warmer on average, and the next question was whether that was natural or due to human agency.

I remember there was a famous climate scientist called Stephen Schneider, dead now, who was one of the first to talk about climate change, and he was eventually elected to the academy of sciences. But his election was opposed by a famous climate scientist whose name I won't mention—but it was not the case that this scientist opposed Schneider's nomination because he was an evil person. It was because he was among those who were not yet convinced that there was a signal behind those fluctuations. Now most Americans, even if not many in our government, are convinced that man-made climate change is real. And then there are still some intelligent people who are not convinced that it is due to human agency, who'd say climate has always changed in the past. The response to that is that the rate of change is a thousand times of what it has been for the last ten thousand—even million—years.

So those are the two reasons why a significant number of Americans are still in denial. Some of them are perfectly nice, intelligent people—but just not convinced.

AD: Thanks to science, we have discovered some global problems that were impossible to perceive in everyday experience, such as the hole in the ozone layer—and we managed to act fairly quickly through the Montreal Agreement, banning CFC gases. Are there further fatal problems unknown to the general public?

JD: The problems of the world are mostly fairly obvious: the first is the use of nuclear weapons, which is quite possible. A second risk is climate change. A third is exhaustion of essential resources, of which phosphate is one. And a fourth would be inequality and the consequences of inequality. If we are to talk about exhaustion of resources, I would talk about fisheries, topsoil, and forests.

AD: Right. I just wanted to emphasize the fact that some of these problems can be very hard to spot and then when you spot them, they can be very hard to communicate convincingly—and then, even if you do, there is a chance that people will go into denial. People's lives are simply too complicated, they need to survive or simply live their lives.

In a perfect world, science would put the relevant facts on the table, the information would be distributed, and the public would make reasonable choices that would be acted on by the political body. But lots of things interfere in this process. You have identified one in your example from Easter Island. The seemingly senseless act of cutting down the last trees could come about because the decision makers isolated themselves from the consequences of their own actions. This is what happens in class societies—the more exposed members of the society suffer from the decisions of the protected upper classes.

JD: Yes. An example can be seen right here where we are now—we are in a wealthy part of Los Angeles. During the time I have lived in Los Angeles, the city has had one major riot: the Rodney King riots. And just before I moved here, they had the Watts riots. Those were riots illustrating isolated communities. The Rodney King riots in 1993 broke out in Downtown Los Angeles, and lots of people got killed. There was concern in wealthier neighborhoods such as this one, Beverly Hills, that the rioters wouldn't just burn poor stores in Downtown Los Angeles, that they would spill out to Beverly Hills—and all the police could do was take these yellow strips of plastic police tape and string them across the boulevards, signaling "don't pass here." Well, the rioters did not come to Beverly Hills then. But you can bet that if trends continue in the United States, there will be more riots and eventually we'll have riots where they pass the yellow strips of plastic.

AD: A parallel case would be the water crisis in Cape Town, South Africa. They are really running out of water, and it's a major city. The affluent areas are drilling their own wells and the water is not distributed evenly—so you get a water war. You could end up with affluent islands that are the only places where you can live—and the rest will be dried out. The problem here is the lack of democracy and justice. Do you think that as climate problems progress, upholding democracy under stress will be the major challenge?

JD: Yes. Climate change has winners and losers. The lottery is not so much whether or not climate change will occur—it is already a fact—but how it will hit you where you are located.

AD: In your book, you mention the Netherlands and how they have a higher degree of environmental consciousness, for the obvious reason that they live under sea level. So, in an ideal democratic process of climate enlightenment, the more you can make people identify with the problem, the more they are ready to act. But, on the other hand, you have the argument that democracies have a problem handling these crises, because democracies are too shortsighted, always thinking short term and too concerned with local issues. Do you see any remedy to those problems?

JD: That is a problem with democracy: that the candidates are concerned with winning elections and so tend to have short horizons. One can react to that by saying that democracy is a terrible form of government and that what we need is a dictatorship, where the dictator knows that he'll be powerful for the next thirty or so years—like Mussolini from 1922 to 1943. He was in power for some 21 years—he was confident that he would stay in power and could afford to take a long-term perspective. Mussolini is an excellent illustration that, yes, dictators can take a long-term perspective—but no one in human history has found a way to make sure that dictators will make good rather than bad decisions.

AD: Are there any among your historical examples of cultures that have risen to the challenge and made very wise and costly long-term maneuvers to avoid threats that were initially difficult to perceive?

JD: In my book I mention Japan and Iceland and Tikopia as examples, and also New Guinea—places with very long-term successful practices. Iceland was colonized only in 830. It has a really fragile environment because the soils are volcanic. It took the settlers nearly two centuries to realize that what works in Norway doesn't necessarily work in Iceland. The heavy glacier soils in Norway are nowhere to be found in Iceland. Once they figured that out, they became much more careful as to the number of sheep they would let out on the pastures. With this knowledge they have been able to live and manage their land for centuries and remain one of the world's most prosperous countries, despite the financial crack ten years ago. Then you have Japan, which has had a state government for two thousand years and which has not had any collapse except for military defeat in World War II. Japan is 76 percent forest; they have done very well in preserving their forests. And then you have Tikopia, an isolated island in the Pacific, that can sustain about one thousand people. It was colonized around 1200 BC. So, the Tikopians have been operating stably for about 3,200 years. In New Guinea there have been people for about 50 000 years and agriculture for seven thousand years—and yes, there has been deforestation—but the New Guinea highlanders realized that there was a problem and figured out how to deal with it through a sustainable kasorina agroforestry—so every village has its kasorina trees, and from these trees they take their wood for fences and building.

These are all societies with long successful track records. One often hears people say: "Well, isn't collapse inevitable? Don't all societies collapse, sooner or later?" No! Some societies make it.

AD: Now, all these societies are isolated—and many of them are islands. Does this have any bearing on their success rates? Isolation can be a boon and it can be a problem.

JD: For a society, isolation can be an advantage—but not if you run out of resources. The Easter Islanders didn't have a second island from which they could get wood. In the past, isolated societies could collapse one by one, without the world even knowing about it. Whereas today we don't have the possibility of isolated collapse, the way we did in the past. Yes, state governments have collapsed in Somalia, and virtually in Afghanistan. Is Somalia worse off than Easter Island was three hundred years ago? There is no way to argue that. Somalia is still getting humanitarian aid. The last outbreak of smallpox was in Somalia—and smallpox was eradicated in Somalia, which means it was eradicated in the whole world. So even if Somalia is isolated enough to suffer from the fact that its state government has collapsed, it's still connected enough to the rest of the world that it can go on and eventually get help.

AD: Interconnectedness seems to be more of a boon than a problem, then, so that in general, it is better to be connected?

JD: Yes and no. The risk of Easter Island–like collapses are unlikely today because we're all so connected. Instead the risk we face today is world collapse—and that is a risk we never faced until recently. When, for instance, the Maya Empire, once the most advanced society in the world, collapsed—no one outside middle America even knew about it. No one else was affected by the collapse. Nowadays, if the most powerful society in the world collapses, then they will take other countries with them.

AD: When societies grow, not only do they experience population growth, but they also get more complicated: there is more division of labor, luxury consumption goes up. Do you see any credible countertendency to these developments, like the "back-to-the-land" movement in the 1970s that tried to restore ideals of self-reliance and self-subsistence?

JD: All modern societies depend on trade. Just as an example: in the news now, there is a lot of talk about the so-called rare earths in China and Malaysia. The United States and Europe are dependent on these rare earths. China in turn is dependent on soybean imports from the United States and Brazil. As living standards go up, the

Chinese are dependent on imports of seafood. All this, together with a thousand other dependencies, makes it unthinkable to talk about a self-sufficient modern society.

AD: So the dream of living in small, protected, and self-sufficient societies is an illusion.

JD: Yes, but it doesn't stop many Americans from trying. Have you heard about the rocket bunkers? In the United States, in the years of the Cold War, we built all these missile bunkers—that is, big holes in the ground. There are very wealthy people who have bought these missile bunkers and converted them into luxury fifteen-story underground apartments surrounded by walls with guards and with stockpiles of stuff to last for months. OK, so they can last for three months. In a missile bunker, even if you are very careful and live simply, you're eventually going to run out of food.

AD: Food is fundamental—and humanity's consumption of food will be decisive to the future of the planet. Wouldn't eating and living more frugally be a natural consequence of the crisis? Even the pioneering critics of the growth economy recommended a plant-based diet. Do you consider this a possible large-scale solution?

JD: How many people do you know who are vegetarians?

AD: Quite a few. The tendency is growing, even if it is limited. Many choose such changes of lifestyle not out of need but also out of a sense of what is right and sustainable. Which leads us to a crucial question: You cite several examples where societies have succeeded in managing common resources by virtue of individuals limiting themselves. This can be conceived of as an extended self-interest—even where the time frames have been very long. Do you think that environmental concerns, which transcend self-interest—let's call them idealist motivations or care for animals and nature—can be a mobilizing factor that makes people give up their luxury consumption?

JD: For most people in the world, moral considerations are themselves a luxury. Just today, this morning, I was talking to someone I collaborate with on my projects in New Guinea and Indonesia. He is making a video trying to convince Indonesians and Indonesians in New Guinea to adopt a more sustainable lifestyle—and the appeal is to idealism. He and I were having a discussion by phone with the filmmaker about whether an appeal to idealism is going to motivate people in New Guinea—and my experience is no! Most people in New Guinea live on a subsistence level, and they want food security, and for that they need money. Therefore, if miners or plantation owners offer them money in the short term, their view is: "Of course I am going to take the money."

AD: Even if this is the situation for most, it should still be possible to advance by influencing the major players directly—the mining companies, the oil companies, and so forth. As a board member and regional manager of WWF for several years, you have worked directly with some of these companies, and you have described how some of them have indeed learned from prior disasters. Other companies seem incapable of learning—or they are not interested. What is the factor that makes some of them learn from their mistakes, and others not?

JD: That is a good question—and one that interests me a lot. The big oil companies differ somewhat in their environmental policies. The biggest of the oil companies, Exxon, is notorious for not taking environmental problems seriously, while Chevron does in many respects. BP does or did in some respects, despite the disaster in the Mexican Gulf in 2010. Why is Exxon blinder than the other companies? Partly because it is larger than the other companies, so that it is more impervious to what's going on. Another reason is the chance factor of the leaders of the company. Exxon has had two presidents in succession who were inclined to dismiss environmental concerns. The CEO of Chevron, on the other hand, is personally concerned about environmental issues. When I was working in Chevron fields in New Guinea I had lots of friends who were workers in the fields of Chevron and they told me what goes on: every week the CEO sends an internet post that goes out to the seventy thousand employees of Chevron—and these posts regularly talk of environmental concerns.

Walmart, which is the biggest retailer in the United States and in the world, up until fifteen years ago had no particular interest in the environment. Then the director, Rob Walton, who loves scuba diving, was taken on a scuba diving trip in eastern Indonesia by the president of Conservation International. Robert was taken to the richest coral reefs in the world where he expected to see sharks every day. Instead he saw two sharks in a week because the coral reefs even in Indonesia are so plundered, among other things for shark fins to be used in shark fin soup. This was a real shock to Walton, and he then played a role in the transformation of Walmart, so that they now have made major efforts to be environmentally sustainable, which they don't talk much about. They have changed their fleet of trucks and made them more fuel efficient, and thereby also saved a lot of money.

AD: Big companies also risk being sued for environmental damage. In Norway, young people are even suing the government for drilling for oil in vulnerable arctic areas. Is this an effective way of addressing the crisis?

JD: It already is a part of the solution. The state of California has a different take on environmental matters and many political matters than the federal government, and so many changes in environmental policies that the federal government is now proposing are being met with lawsuits by the state of California. But the federal government has also considered suing the state of California. There are lawsuits both ways.

AD: So we see a process where society is learning from history through institutional change. Those who experience or fear environmental destruction report back to governments and decision makers. Do you see in these processes a cause for optimism? Are we learning fast, not fast enough—or way too slowly to get a grip on the challenges?

JD: I would describe myself as an optimist, as my wife and I decided to have children. That means something like this: I see the chances as 51 percent that thirty years from now you'll find a world worth living in, and 49 percent that you wouldn't want to be alive. Are we doing enough? No, of course we're not doing enough. Are we doing some things? Yes, we are doing some things.

I am optimistic when it comes to international agreements and treatises. For instance, oil used to be transported in single hull tankers. If you got a hole in the hull, your oil would spill out. About twenty years ago, an agreement was reached that all oil tankers should have a double hull. Oil leaks have been reduced drastically. There is also significant progress in health—smallpox has been wiped out through a coordinated international effort. There was a worldwide effort to wipe out rinderpest, a horrible disease of livestock. There are efforts to eliminate river blindness and river worm. Those are achievements that give me hope.

AD: Steven Pinker has argued alongside yourself that there is a tendency to decreased violence as societies become industrialized—even if some people would like to think that primitive societies are quite idyllic and peaceful.

JD: Yes, some people like to think that—people who have never seen a primitive society.

AD: The same Steven Pinker is concerned with re-establishing the enlightenment faith in moral progress, and has lately talked a lot about how there is actually a lot of progress in dealing with environmental issues, to the effect that pessimism is now becoming a major problem, because it forces people into denial instead of generating efforts to deal with the problem. What do you think about this?

JD: As a practical issue, it is true that if you are too pessimistic, then you share your pessimism with other people. If I convince you that the world is going to be ruined, why should anybody make any effort? You've got to give people hope. Even if you don't believe it yourself, you've still got to give them hope.

AD: What about technological solutions? Can new technologies save us?

JD: New technologies inevitably produce new problems that often can't be properly predicted. Some people say technology will solve our problems. That usually means that they hope that some magic technology can solve our problems without us taking the environmental concerns seriously. I'm not one of those who think that technology can provide much hope for solving our problems.

AD: So we come back to the choices we make in organizing our societies—and in this respect the steadily growing class of luxury consumers seems to be a problem. At the same time, inequality is a problem in itself. Is it a bigger problem than both population growth and the growth in consumption?

JD: Inequality is one of the big problems, and in the long run it's not viable. Because poor countries in direct and indirect ways make trouble for richer countries. This is a problem we could actually do something about, since there are many ways to help poorer countries. There is also wasteful consumption, particularly in the United States. The only reason why luxury cars and gas cost less than half what they do in Europe, in countries like Norway and Germany, is that we don't tax these goods. We could have reduced our emissions significantly in the U.S. if we deployed similar means of regulation.

AD: Equality concerns the problem of a balanced sharing of burdens and benefits among people. What about fairness to nature? As a passionate bird-watcher and biologist, don't you sometimes feel that humanity's crisis and questions of injustice will constantly push concerns for people to the foreground, and the survival of other species to the background?

JD: An equivalent question would be do I care more about one son than the other. I care about the future of human societies, but I also care about my beloved birds.

RESTARTING THE WORLD SYSTEM

with Bernard Stiegler

Bernard Stiegler (1952–2020) was a French philosopher and activist, best known for his rereading of the philosophy of technology. Stiegler was also known as a critic of consumer society and of automation. He wrote extensively about digital networks and how they affect the individual and society. He also wrote about ecology and climate in conjunction with the concept of the Anthropocene, which he understood as an unsustainable state we must move out of as quickly as possible.

Stiegler's most famous work is the multivolume *La Technique et le Temps I-III* [Technics and Time I-III] (1994–2001). Besides presenting a general theory about technology and the way it characterizes the human world, it draws up a broadly constructed social critique. Stiegler's focus ranges from the psychological and philosophical, to the anthropological, aesthetic, and economic. Stiegler develops what he calls a "general organology," examining the relationship between the human body and mind, and how they work with the artificial organs of technology. He presents technology from a pharmacological point of view, as a medicine that can also act as a poison. In later books, such as *The Neganthropocene* (2018) and *The Age of Disruption* (2018), the impact of technology on the biosphere and the human mind emerges as a central theme.

In what was to become his last book, *Qu'appelle-t-on Panser? T2: La leçon de Greta Thunberg* [What Is Caring in Thinking? The Lesson of Greta Thunberg] (2020), Stiegler deepens his discussion of what it means to care for the world, and how we are to understand the justified anger of the younger generation of climate protesters.

Anders Dunker: In our time, both nature and culture seem to be in radical imbalance—internally and with respect to each other. A great deal of this imbalance can be traced back to an acceleration of technological development—which intervenes in nature, society, and the individual's body and mind. Since you wrote your first philosophical work on technology, you've constantly come back to the fact that technology is a double-edged sword. In what way is this the case today?

Bernard Stiegler: We must understand that technology in general—flint tools, a hammer, writing, radio, the atomic bomb—are what the ancient Greeks called *pharmaka*. They are both poisonous and curative. But in order to make them curative, you need to limit their possibilities; you must create laws for prescribing their practice, their use. The more dangerous the technology, the more vital the regulation. For example, nuclear weapons are regulated by international treaties, and, when you think about it, most technologies are regulated in one way or another. Now, who is doing the regulating? A legitimated power—and for a long time this power was the state. And now, because of the network community and globalization, the government's control over technology is by and large over—and herein lies the problem. What kind of control over technology and its adverse effects can we organize in the twenty-first century? This is all the more important since we live in an era where the Anthropocene may already be in its decisive final phase, and where, for example, the Intergovernmental Panel on Climate Change says we have ten years to save the situation.

AD: If the Anthropocene is defined as the age where humans have thrown the biosphere and geophysical systems out of balance, it might be said that the cause is not humans as such, but rather technological disruption, which interrupts and replaces the slow adaptations of more original systems. What connection do you see between the disruption of the atmosphere through the burning of fossil fuels, a process that began with the taming of fire, and the current disruption of human life through digital technologies, which can be traced back to the invention of writing? How do these two developments interact? What is the connection between the disruption of what Félix Guattari calls the three ecologies—our mental, social, and natural environments?

BS: Now you speak of disruption in such a wide sense that it begins with hominization, and the transformation of the biosphere into what the Russian geochemist Vladimir Vernadsky calls the technosphere. This first disruption was not at all conscious and played out at a very slow pace, which made it appear natural and almost unnoticeable. What we call disruption today is something much more recent. The second disruption came with the industrial revolution at the end of the nineteenth century in England, with the massive extraction of coal and the first steam engines—and this became the beginning of what we have come to call the Anthropocene. Then comes a third period, which is the one we normally associate with disruption, beginning with digital technologies, and especially with the so-called Moore's law, describing the accelerating development of microchips and processing capacity. This disruption sped up when the internet was made available to everyone on the planet in 1993 via the World Wide Web. In the course of these threefold processes, ecosystems and the biosphere as a whole have been severely changed, and with them society. Like the historian Arnold Toynbee, I emphasize that, in the past, society was organized to resist the toxic effects of new technologies. The church, for instance, established a series of measures to regulate technology—so that it would be used in accordance with nature—which for the Christian church was the same as God's creation.

As capitalism established itself, especially in countries where the church was reformed, many of these practices were suspended in a process which Max Weber calls rationalization and which the German philosopher Peter Sloterdijk calls disinhibition—a systematic removal of limits and inhibitions that had been carefully established through moral customs. The new social systems which emerged from the eighteenth century to the twentieth century brought technological changes that often entailed destruction of both societies and nature. Yet this period also produced new forms of solidarity with a secular basis. In the spirit of the Enlightenment all of this was called progress.

AD: And then the technological changes began accelerating further...

BS: Towards the end of the twentieth century, digital technologies appeared quite suddenly, and we saw a whole new level of disruption. Now the technological disruption of society and nature has become ubiquitous. Even if disruptions in a certain sense can be said to be as old as technology itself, the digital revolution has provoked something new and different, both because of the enormous speed with which its technologies change and because of the enormous scale on which they are playing out. We ought to remember that until the beginning of the 1980s, TV networks were territorial or regional simply because the signal had to be relayed by masts with a limited range. With digital technology this has changed completely, especially with GPS technology and what I call the "exosphere," which consists of satellites.

AD: How do you envision the disruption of satellite technology? What did it lead to?

BS: Social, economic, and political decision-making processes were, for instance, short-circuited by this technology. It was the beginning of what is now called platform capitalism. And, on this level, we have something new which completely disrupts the political organization of society, which, for us, began in the seventh century BC in Greece, and then spread via Rome and the Catholic Church to the West as a whole—first Europe, and then America. All this is completely destroyed now by such an evolution, and I myself consider that such a destruction is extremely dangerous because it is a destruction of the regulation of the toxicity of the pharmakon.

AD: Since you began writing about the attention economy at the beginning of the 2000s, it has become increasingly clear that attention is a resource which can be exploited and plundered just like natural resources. Maybe we can see the psychosocial sphere and the biosphere as two ecologies, each with its own metabolism, its own circulation of energy. How can we muster the mental resources of will and motivation required to solve our environmental problems, when we have an economy that pillages and extracts values from these resources and which captures and ensnares our precious attention?

BS: Here we should refer to Nicholas Georgescu-Roegen, who was a pupil of Schumpeter. Georgescu-Roegen had very good knowledge of the works of Alfred Lotka, Norbert Wiener, and Vernadsky. He says that the economy of consumer capitalism is by necessity self-destructive because it is based on formalisms that are themselves based on the physics of Newton. We are not, however, living in Newton's world, but instead in the world of thermodynamics and under the law of entropy. So, he said that we have to change the economy. I have tried to reinterpret his work: it was in 1971 that he wrote his book *The Entropy Law and the Economic Process,* and I have tried to show that the real question is to reinterpret Alfred Lotka. In a very important text published in 1945, in the journal *Human Biology*—a short text of twenty pages—Lotka offers a very powerful interpretation of the human phenomenon. In addition to our organic organs, humans have artificial, inorganic organs. They can give rise to an increase in entropy or to negentropy. Now, if we understand that, we must also remember what was said by Karl Marx, namely that industrialization necessarily produces a process of proletarianization, where work is transformed into labour. This proletarianization is, in fact, the destruction of knowledge. We have to reconsider the industrial economy from a new point of view, which is what I call "hyper-industrialization," in which the problem is to give work to people. First because they need money so that they are able to consume, and, if we don't give them money, the economy will inevitably fail because it will lead to an economic crisis. A new problem of distribution is opened with the process of automation, which is a huge problem, pointed out by MIT a decade ago. The other problem is that the economy should be reorganized completely according to a new goal: that of limiting entropy and increasing negentropy, that is, energy conservation and stability. For that, we need to create a new form of accounting. Because today, if you look, for example, at corporate accounting, an increase in entropy may well be considered to be good for a company. This is extremely dangerous for the company itself, but also for the globe.

AD: So, on the one hand, we try to keep up the consumption to save the economy; but, at the same time, consumption must be reduced to save the planet. How do we resolve this paradox?

BS: First, I would like to recall the real meaning of economy. Initially, to economize meant to avoid wastefulness. Avoiding the destruction of things. You must economize because the world is limited. You cannot consume everything. You must use it and consume it in an intelligent way. You must defer consumption and limit it. This economizing was destroyed by consumer capitalism, which is sometimes called, in France, diseconomy, that is—an anti-economy, a contradiction with economy. For this reason, we have to invent a new form of economy—an economy which is industrial, but which aims not to increase entropy: which employs new technologies, while giving workers the opportunity to increase their knowledge instead of being supplanted by automated systems that proletarize them, in the sense that they are reduced to instruments.

AD: Extraction and exploitation seem to be consequences of the disruption of nature and of our inner environment—social interaction and our mental and bodily life. In both cases, the development is difficult to change or even halt once changes to the system have occurred. Is it possible to predict the toxic consequences of technologies, or do we have to resign ourselves to discovering the problems after the damage has already been done?

BS: I think it is always possible to anticipate toxicity. I say that because I myself anticipated that those technologies were toxic a long time ago. For example, in 2004, I published a book called *Symbolic Misery*, and in the third chapter, I said that there would be social networks. At this time social networks barely existed. You didn't have a smartphone, but I considered the prospects and said that this will occur—because it's a necessary part of the evolution of technical systems. And I said that if we don't regulate it, then we will have lots of problems.

AD: Which problems are the most pressing?

BS: First, and most general—and this may come as a surprise—the increase of entropy and the entropic evolution of society, which is a destruction of society. This was anticipated by Norbert Wiener in 1948, a year before he had even created the concept of cybernetics, the general theory of self-regulating feedback systems. And he said, be careful: cybernetics is necessary but extremely dangerous. For example, he said that cybernetics will evolve into networks and these networks will produce a new kind of fascism. This is what has happened.

AD: He also said we will have to solve these problems at a very inconvenient point in our history, where we will not have the resources or means to counteract them. We still need to unpack what lies in this concept of entropy. He talks about it in nature, in the universe, how the tendency goes toward the dissipation and irreversible expenditure of energy—a burnt-out state drained of energetic potential. But Wiener also wrote that noise and meaninglessness is a form of entropy, while any successful communication, in effect, is the opposite—negentropy.

BS: In human life, negentropy is knowledge. And when I say knowledge, I do not mean information. For me, information is not knowledge at all, but rather something that tends to destroy knowledge, since too much information acts as noise. Sometimes you need information and you can use information to produce knowledge, but knowledge is a transformation of information. This is a decisive point, and again I have to refer to Marx: the most important aspect of what he calls proletarization is the loss of knowledge, the understanding of the work that you perform, the loss of knowledge about how to live. Since the end of the eighteenth century, which was also the beginning of the Anthropocene, we have been subjected to a process of proletarianization, that is, a loss of knowledge, and this process of proletarianization first affected the manual workers, then it affected the technicians, then the engineers, and today top management itself—even the top management of states. Why? Because everything became machinic, and machinism later became informational machinism based on computer science and computation. That said, I am not against calculation. I practice computer science, and in my institute, we develop many digital devices and pieces of software. Still, I contend that if you reduce everything to calculation, you increase entropy.

AD: So how can we counteract this process that outstrips people's knowledge and their know-how, even when it comes to the question of how to live life itself? And how can this help us to solve environmental problems, to care for life and the natural world around us?

BS: For example, I launched a project in the north of Paris, in a territory with 400,000 inhabitants, for building—in the context of the Olympic Games—a new kind of building made out of clay. Because in Paris, in the soil, we have lots of clay—and this is considered to be bad—because the concrete industry says it is better to build with concrete. As it turns out, clay is much better than concrete—for thermal qualities. So we are trying to transform that by reinventing the work of manual workers—this is a process of deproletarianization—but we do that also for many other workers—car mechanics, for example. Like Stuttgart, Paris decided that by 2023, diesel motors will not be allowed to enter Paris, because of pollution. In 2030, the same will apply to all kinds of combustion engines. In France, we will then have thirty million cars that will be immobilized by these decisions. And those cars are not in a bad state. So, you can use them, but you must transform them into electric cars. If you follow the industry of metallurgy with robotization and completely proletarianized workers, they are incapable of doing that, so we have to completely reinvent the work done by mechanics.

AD: Inventing is more inspiring than protesting. In some of your books, like *The Decadence of Industrial Democracies*, you describe protests as reactive and dangerously close to nihilism. Invention may be more stimulating, yet many people really despair over the inaction of politicians. Greta Thunberg has protested against her parents' generation, saying they have done too little, that they should panic, that they are too complacent, that they constantly postpone solving the problems. Extinction Rebellion in London is mobilizing emotions like anger and grief, disrupting traffic to bring attention to global warming and the mass extinction of nonhuman species. How do you relate to these kinds of protests?

BS: I am of course very happy to see that young people in general are raising these questions in the first place. That is extremely good. Now our responsibility, the older generations—teachers, scientists, lawyers, also managers of companies, etc.—is to reply to such questions and to propose something really new. This is why we have created with lawyers, artists, scientists, etc., something that we have called Geneva 2020.

AD: What are you hoping to achieve?

BS: Our project was presented in Geneva on January 10, 2020. The day was the centenary of the founding of the League of Nations. The background was obviously the First World War and the aim was to avoid a new world war. And it was a complete failure, as we all know. Only nineteen years later a new war happened. After this Second World War, the United Nations was created, and this organization wasn't a complete failure, because it helped to avoid a nuclear Third World War, which is extremely important, yet it failed to address a new kind of war, which is the global economic war. I myself tried to calculate the destruction engendered by this war, which really got going in the 1980s, with the destruction of what we can call the Keynesian state and the welfare state by the conservative and ultraliberal, neoliberal discourse, which reopened a war, but a war by economic means. And this war destroyed many things. First, the destruction of the environment was extremely accelerated, jobs were destroyed, many countries were destroyed, ruined, even banks. If you look at the European states today, they are ruined; they are not at all capable of refinancing the banks if there is a new crash. And this is what will happen. Everybody knows that it will happen. All this is a result of a destruction by an economic war. Today we have to decide a new peace, an economic peace, in which we should, for example, put a stop to the extraction of value by shareholders at such a level, for example, 15 percent a year. That is completely destroying the economy. Everybody knows that. Even managers know that.

AD: How can we end what you call the economic war if those who try to limit themselves thereby risk ending up as losers?

BS: First we have to negotiate an economic peace treaty, which we are developing—and which is presented in the Geneva 2020 book titled *Bifurquer* [Bifurcate]. Next, we must reorganize the economy and base it on the struggle against entropy. We must reorganize work so that we can give new work and new competences to people. This is what we have been experimenting with in Plaine Commune: contributory income, which is not at all a salary or unemployment wages. Instead, you give money to people to develop their knowledge. For everything. Education of infants, football, science, the building of new kinds of buildings made of clay. But it is a conditional income. You can get it only if you are able to find what we call an intermittent job for three months to create value from your knowledge. So it is a process and works differently than universal basic income. Ideas like these can contribute to a new model for capitalist development. Perhaps the result will be something other than capitalism. I don't know—it is not up to me. Such a transition will be an experimental transition. And we must involve societies and countries whose experiences are the results of the experiments of others—people living on islands or in regions made uninhabitable by climate change. Toxic technologies create disruption and lead to increased entropy in a number of different areas. That is why we have established a group of mathematicians—like Giuseppe Longo—lawyers such as Alain Supiot, very well known, too—and people like Geert Lovink, the social networking activist from Amsterdam. In the Internation project, I work with biologists and physicists, specialists on taxes and international law, internet activists, and many other experts, together with my friends Yuk Hui, Dan Ross, and others. We propose a program to respond to the IPCC's report with a method, scientific statements, but also with debates and practical laboratories—because today the problem is that we are in a state of emergency. We must work fast to develop a new methodology capable of being applied to science and to society. All of this, if you will, is also a response to the girl from Sweden who says that we must now address these problems. We are trying to do it.

AD: This sounds like a Plan A for the planet, which is just what we need. But how are such radical propositions received by those in power?

BS: Of course, we also try to bring banks along with us, the managers of big companies and so on, and there are many people in those positions who believe that the situation is extremely dangerous. They cannot say that openly, because if they do so, the shareholders will tell them, "We don't want you to manage our business." So they don't say it. They cannot say it.

AD: This might be a good example of what you call "disinhibition through reason," since the practice of the companies is decided by calculated gain and nothing else, making it a pseudo-automatic system of predictable responses. A short-sighted rationality like this leads to denial of the destructive effects that follow, which you describe as no less than a systematic madness...

BS: Again, when everything is reduced to calculation, you increase entropy. The statement is also valid on a mathematical level, as von Bertalanffy explained in his general system theory. This is of course the problem of information. What we call information today is always calculable information. Information is defined by its capacity to be calculated. Now negentropy is never calculable within the system where it happens. So here we find a contradiction, which Immanuel Kant actually discussed at the end of the eighteenth century, since this was the question at stake in his *Critique of Pure Reason*. What we need today is a new critique of what I call "impure reason." Whereas for Kant, reason was pure, for me reason is pharmacological, which means that we must distinguish between poisonous and curative uses of reason. It is impure.

AD: All of these considerations are very abstract. How do you go about communicating them to a wider audience? You work with mathematicians, you reference the history of philosophy and speak of entropy and negentropy, but these aren't everyday notions, at least not yet. Do you experience a problem of communication as you combine abstract theories with social practice?

BS: I understand what you mean, but if people get confused because they don't know what entropy is, you could also say, "But you don't understand how your smartphone works—yet you use it every day." So we should rather try to win back people's confidence in science—and move beyond the current state of a post-truth society—especially with respect to climate change denial.

AD: In one of your latest books, *The Age of Disruption*, you describe the post-truth era itself as a form of entropy—a dissolution of systems of knowledge and of communication. What is the core of this problem?

BS: The posttruth era has its origin in a loss of confidence and a destruction of trust. When we have a system that is fundamentally dysfunctional, it creates discredit and disbelief on all levels, not only for Trump voters, for example. So we must relearn how to communicate, and that means to communicate honestly also about scientific questions and work on a new model that can be made concrete for society. We are denying the problem of climate change, as we deny other problems, when we don't see any real possibility of changing the situation. We need to sleep at night. We need to keep going. Since it is unbearable to be thinking of these incredibly dangerous situations—which affect everyone, our friends, ourselves, our families, our societies—we go into denial. In the absence of a real solution, denial appears to be the most efficient way of dealing with it, and this is what Trump has done, this is what the managers of big companies do, just like people do it in their everyday lives. On the other hand, if you can present a plan—like we do in Paris—and if it is possible to communicate that the plan is workable, it can have an extremely positive effect. The possibility of a solution makes it possible to take in the problem.

AD: When the World Wide Web was introduced in 1993, and when social media appeared ten years later, the general sentiment was optimism: We would all be part of a global village, we would freely exchange information and solve our problems together. Plans and social reforms like the one you describe would appear spontaneously. Now, we have entered a much darker epoch, where social media is an integrated part of capitalism, led by gigantic companies like Google and Facebook, who harvest our data and predict our actions. Do you see any good way to tackle these problems? Can the systems be changed or regulated? Are there any alternatives?

BS: I work on these problems with my colleague Yuk Hui, who leads an international network of scientists in the intersection between philosophy and technology. Five years ago, we developed a new concept for social networks at our institute. Plaine Commune is a laboratory also for this concept. The decisive problem—which is simultaneously technological, political, and economical—is locality. Today, digital social networks contribute to the destruction of locality—and this is extremely dangerous.

AD: How does this happen?

BS: It means that regulation is short-circuited and undone on all levels. It means that people living in the deserts of Algeria are given the same views on life and the world as people from Norway or Sweden, for example. But in Algeria, you are in the Sahara. You can't live like you do in Sweden. It is impossible. And it is also not necessary. Because if I like to go to Sweden or Nigeria, it is because it is different. But these differences were destroyed by extractivism, as it is called in the critique of consumer capitalism. And we have to re-evaluate these localities. Why? Because an economy of negentropy is necessarily an economy of locality. Why? Because negentropic systems are always local. As Schrödinger and Wiener point out, what is negentropic in one place can be entropic in another and vice versa. So the economy of negentropy is necessarily localized. We have to recreate local social networks. And those local systems must be open—not like the communities dreamed of by the far right who are becoming racist and closed. Not at all. It is exactly the contrary. But the reason why, for example, in Finland you see the far right having electoral success is that we are denying the real question. The real question is not migration. It can be a question, but the real question is that localities are being destroyed economically, culturally, and cognitively—and this is making life impossible, or at least difficult, as it puts life and diversity at risk.

AD: In which ways?

BS: An illustrative example is all the languages that are dying out, and that we are striving to preserve. Today, English is the world language, and that is fine. A thousand years ago, it was Latin, the language of the clerics. Three hundred years ago, French was the language of diplomacy. Now we have Globish, which is practiced by everybody. I think it is necessary, like in the ancient Greek polis, for example, where you had the Koine, which was the language for everybody, to protect the dialects and the different languages. Now we are destroying that diversity, and this must be avoided, because this diversity is what produces negentropy.

AD: So if for now we equate negentropy with long-term sustainability, can we say that diversity is necessary for social and psychological systems, just as it is in the ecosystems of the biological world? How can we protect diversity when the net brings everyone into the same market with the same agents and the same conditions?

BS: On a more general level, we have to change the programs and networks, making them more adapted to local conditions. With Yuk Hui, I have worked with engineers and big telephone and internet companies, such as

Orange and Dassault Systems, designing a new kind of platform that is localized and where you produce value through proximity. If you want to create an ecological economy, you have to value and favour the local. The question is how this is to be done in an integrated and systematic way. Europe is rich in diversity and consists of a patchwork of localities—Norway, Sweden, Denmark, Germany, Belgium, France, Italy, Spain: they are all localities and this represents a certain kind of wealth. This is also the reason why there are such good mathematicians and engineers in Europe, because of this diversity—and a cultural heritage if you will. I think this is entirely possible.

AD: In nature, loss of biodiversity is not only caused by capitalist pressure on habitats and so-called extractivism, that is, the understanding of nature as a resource: the problem is also that everything is increasingly exposed to everything else, poisons and parasites are spread by our movements and activities and are diffused around the globe. This is also valid for economies: they are exposed to competition, and increasingly activities are outsourced and outcompeted. How can local enclaves and markets be protected against the world market? Norwegian fish is sometimes processed and packed in China, before it is shipped back for sale in Norway.

BS: Such situations are only possible because of negative externalities. The social economic costs are far higher than the production costs for the company. If you take into consideration the expenditure of fossil fuel and the release of carbon between Norway and China, the equation is completely different. So it is what I call "economic war." Warriors of this kind are destroying everything around themselves. And it is not at all taken into account. So we have to find a new form of accounting in order to create circuits that are negentropic. This is in everyone's interest. I have spent a lot of time in China lately, and everybody there is now concerned with climate change and pollution. They know that they must solve this problem. They are the ones with the strongest interest. They have entered a very prosperous era. But this could be destroyed in the next ten years, and they understand that now. So the challenge is to open a new negotiation. And this negotiation must not be based on credits for emissions of carbon dioxide, since the creation of such a market has proven extremely dangerous. Instead, we must redefine the very basis of the economy. And it is possible because it is everyone's problem and hence everyone's obligation. You know, even Elon Musk will have problems with that; even Peter Thiel will have to deal with the problem of climate change. So the challenge is to find a rational way that is tenable and that is also interesting.

AD: What do you mean when you say that it also has to be interesting? Why is this important?

BS: You know, the human being is an animal that needs to have an interest—that is, an intellectual interest. When I say "intellectual," I do not only mean philosophy or science or mathematics, it is also interesting to play chess, to play football. If you fish, and you know how to fish trout, it is very intellectual. What is interesting is what draws you in. To look at someone fishing trout—I saw it myself in Siberia—it is extremely interesting. Today we are all becoming couch potatoes, with the smartphone, the beer, and streaming media and social networks; but people are not happy with that, not at all. The youth, for example, are completely despairing. We know that in Palo Alto, Silicon Valley, the suicide rate of young people is the highest in all of America. All those young people, they are the children of rich businesspeople, they have access to everything, but still they despair. So it is not only a problem for poor people living in India but also for the rich. The problem is to find a way out of all this, which is also rational. What I mean by "rational" here is something deeper than being clever, it is about creating a future. A future is something different than a becoming. A becoming is simply what happens, random events, or the statistically probable.

AD: What happens when we are left to the probable, as you comment at the end of your book *The Neganthropocene*, is usually dismal. The odds are not on our side. The most probable, it seems, is that we will not manage the environmental problems, and that politically we will slide further and deeper into barbarism, chaos, indifference, and resignation.

BS: In the worst case we end up not only in passive indifference, but also become more aggressive and murderous. We see this tendency in the mass shootings in the U.S. and other places. In France it has manifested differently, in the demonstrations of the Gilets Jaunes. But the problem is the same. In China, a great part of the population is in a state of depression. I think most people readily acknowledge that the world situation and the complex challenges we are faced with are extremely desperate.

AD: But, on the other hand, there is hope—and I like what you wrote about hope always being a hope for the improbable. And what you call negentropy could also be described as something improbable, which is nonetheless possible. Norbert Wiener says almost the same thing, that life itself is very improbable. The stuff we are made of is miraculous, so to speak. And he repeats a simple example that inspires hope: With a negligible expenditure of energy, information can be transferred in such a way that it makes a difference and creates negative entropy. For instance, the information in the genome of a seed can transform soil, sunlight, and water into a tree, which in turn binds energy. Information about climate change can be spread to people in countries across the globe and have started changing people's behaviors and our technologies. Is that what we are hoping for, a sort of material miracle? A change that spreads and crystallizes and that transforms the world and our lives?

BS: Yes, absolutely: What you are talking about is what Gilbert Simondon calls "amplification," and this is the key to the negentropic way for humans. Our technologies are really miraculous. And for a long time, since Leonardo da Vinci, it was a dream—"I would like to fly." Four centuries later, we are flying. It is miraculous. Life, as you say, as Wiener says, it is miraculous. Everything that is interesting is miraculous. You say that it is difficult to explain entropy and negentropy to people, but no, I don't think it is. You can simply tell them: "Let's have some tea." You serve them the tea. And then you wait and you say, "You see: ten minutes ago it was very hot, now it is not so hot."

AD: The tea has gotten colder, but your own body temperature has miraculously remained the same?!

BS: Exactly! This is easy to explain to people. You must always assume that people are interested, intelligent, and that they have a good will. If you decide that they are stupid and have a bad spirit, then they become stupid, just like you assumed.

AD: Yet, you also address stupidity as a very real problem of our times. You write about this in your book *Automatic Society*. How more and more processes in our society are becoming automatic, and that what disappears is the space, the pause, to wait, dream, deliberate and create new alternatives. The result is stupidity?

BS: I have already mentioned proletarization, how knowledge apparently is just made superfluous but is in fact destroyed by automated processes. Psychologically it is not only your intelligence and knowledge that are affected, but also your will and your desire—your motivations and your goals. You go to Amazon because you want something, and they use your so-called friends, and it enables Amazon to suggest many things that you didn't have any wish to buy, but in the end you will want them. It is extremely efficient when it comes to user profiling, predicting, and anticipating your behaviors, your will, your desire, so we become more predictable in turn. It is short-circuiting what you want to do, taking control of your behavior and—in the end—you feel that it is not your behavior, and you become more like an automaton than yourself. This is the feeling of many people today, who experience the smartphone as extremely addictive. They admit: "I use it as an addict, yet I continue to do it. It is destroying my life, now my life is on the network." I don't think it is possible to go on managing a company like Amazon with such a malaise. Short-circuiting your will, your projects, what Husserl calls "protentions," which are your own anticipations of the future.

Your own psychological protentions are hijacked by automatic protentions. How? Because computers send messages two million times faster than does your own brain and nervous system. We end up in an addictive, toxic, destructive situation in which we are disindividuated—to use the phrase of Gilbert Simondon. People lose their feeling of existence—lose their grip and disappear to themselves. This also destroys wealth and creates poverty. Because real wealth is always constituted by negentropic knowledge, knowledge about how to generate and retain energy. So we have to change that and figure out ways of making calculations and software that increases the will and the wealth of knowledge.

AD: At the end of the 1880s, Nietzsche describes this situation, saying that once we have a common economic management of the earth, which he sees as something inevitable, humans will find themselves serving this machinery, as ever more adapted gears, making individual will and values increasingly redundant...

BS: I recently came out with a book about Nietzsche [*Qu'appelle-t-on panser?*], where I attempt to show how Nietzsche was extremely impressed by entropy and the heat death of the universe. But, at this time, he did not know the concept of negentropy. I try to show that what he called the "eternal return" was a concept of negentropy. The first one to understand the stakes of that was Bergson, who was an eager reader of Nietzsche, and who anticipated negentropy. And then Freud anticipated negentropy. And then Schrödinger produced the concept of negentropy. So I think it is possible today to remobilize Nietzsche through a concept of negentropy that he did not have access to himself.

AD: Nietzsche also saw the role of the philosopher as that of a doctor of culture. Can we understand human will as a renewable resource and the starting point for a new health?

BS: The challenge is to give a good diagnosis of the situation we are in, and then to find an effective cure. I think both are necessary and possible.

THE PLANTS, THE PLANET, AND US

with Sandra Díaz

Sandra Díaz (b. 1961) is an Argentinian ecologist. She is cofounder of the Global Communal Plant Trait Initiative (TRY), which systematically collects information on plant traits. She has developed models to arrange the world's plants based on functional features, such as the size of their leaves and seeds, their height, and whether they grow slowly or quickly. As coexistence with humans has proved to be a determining factor in how well many plant species cope, she has initiated interdisciplinary projects with social scientists. The goal is to understand what a wide range of social groups want from the local environment, what they appreciate about the ecosystems they connect with, and how they shape them.

Díaz is one of the world's most cited and talked about environmental scientists and has collaborated with the UN-backed Intergovernmental Science-Policy Platform on Biodiversity and Ecosystem Service, which compiles reports with the Intergovernmental Panel on Climate

Change. As an ecologist with an interdisciplinary approach to the issue of biodiversity, she helps us uncover our direct and indirect impacts on nature.

Anders Dunker: From where did you get your passion for plants? And how has this passion influenced your work with local communities and the ties they have to local nature?

Sandra Díaz: I have had a passion for plants for as long as I can remember. When I was a little girl I used to prowl around in the garden of my home, or in wastelands near my house when I managed to escape, looking at the plants. I have always had a passion for animals, too, but I decided to focus mostly on plants for research. I guess this is because my emotional attachment to animals is too strong, and because I do not have the patience required to study them in the wild. Animals, unless they are the sessile animals of coral reefs and intertidal habitats, move a lot, they are not easy to find. While plants, as the biologist John Harper famously said, are just sitting there, waiting to be counted.

AD: But there is more to it than counting and sorting: You also have to find common traits and functions. Concerning your approach to biology, you say you recognize two forbears: Theophrastus, who was a colleague of Aristotle and who was also teacher to Alexander the Great, and J. P. Grime, your own mentor. Do these two biologists have anything in common? What makes you mention these two in particular?

SD: What they have in common is that they both go for simple, general patterns underlying more superficial complexity. They could be described in today's parlance as "lumpers." They like understanding the world using simple, general categories, rather than getting lost in detailed intricacies. I have the same predilection. I have the same predilection, I am a much better "lumper" than "splitter."

AD: Theories of adaptation must be important for the understanding of biological life in a rapidly changing world. How can a systematic theory of the adaptation of plants help us predict and chart the loss of biodiversity we are experiencing today?

SD: If one derives general "rules" of what plants "do," in the sense of how they respond to environmental factors and how they affect other organisms and the functioning of the ecosystem, one can start to anticipate how species and ecosystems react to a changing world, including, of course, human-driven large-scale changes in climate, land use, etc. It holds the promise of making more sense of natural communities, of not having to model each species individually, or to assume all species as identical. The first is unfeasible, the second strongly distorts what happens in real ecosystems.

AD: Your sympathy for J. P. Grimes's approach led to you working with him. How did you proceed in your research?

SD: He influenced me deeply, in going for the bone of things. Also as an experimentalist. I had never done experimental community ecology until then. And he is a superb experimentalist: he has always managed to go for really fundamental questions with very simple, but extremely ingenious experimental setups. In my case, we built microcosms of plant communities and watched how they did under ambient and elevated CO_2 baseline and nutrient-rich soils. It was technologically extremely simple, nothing fancy, but we got really good results. Then we escalated to mesocosms with not only plants, but also herbivores. We teamed up with a PhD student of Phil's, Lauchlan Fraser, who is now a professor in Canada. We used greenflies and snails and asked whether different combinations of atmospheric CO_2 and soil nutrients influenced not only plant communities but also the herbivores that fed on them. It was great fun, not only scientifically, also logistically. I used a cement mixer to mix many hundreds of kilograms of soil. And we needed a lot of snails. We almost got arrested a couple of times for climbing stonewalls and getting into the shrubbery in search of snails all around the city of Sheffield.

AD: E. O. Wilson has complained in his books that research programs in molecular biology get all the financing and produce detailed, verifiable, and often marketable findings, whereas ecological fieldwork is slow, time-consuming, and less lucrative. Is this still the case? Are people's movements and volunteers needed? Do you have examples of successful programs to mobilize people to collect data and protect species?

SD: Indeed, ecological work, particularly primary fieldwork, is still comparatively slow, time-consuming, physically uncomfortable, and very often not commercially attractive in the short term. But it is absolutely crucial. And yes, partnerships with citizens and other social actors are needed, more now than ever.

AD: Are the number of "biophiles"—people who deeply loves nature and put it at the center of their lives—a constant fraction of our societies, a subculture on par with other hobbies or vocations—or do you see people waking up to not only the threat to their own safety, but also to the preciousness of nature and the need to engage? What are the chances that a form of biophilia and biocentrism can get really widespread and become a foundation of our cultures and our civilization?

SD: The first thing is not thinking about "saving biodiversity" as some kind of altruistic pursuit. We need to think of regaining our birthright of a fulfilling, flourishing relationship with nature. This is not just about recycling bottles, refusing plastic bags at the supermarket, or composting your orange peels. These are all fine and necessary, of course, but not enough by far. We are talking a much deeper change in the social narratives that we enact every day, as individual and societies. The world is not just going down ecologically—it is also unsustainably unfair. It is not only about what we do to the rest of the planet. It is also what we do to each other in these times where the fabric of life is becoming undone.

AD: You have become known for your repeated use of this metaphor, the fabric of life. In which sense is life like a fabric? And why do you find this metaphor particularly useful?

WARP

WEFT →

SD: The fabric of life is simply life on Earth, including all the organisms around and inside us. I like it because you can analyze it at different levels. As I said above, you can go for the fundamental principles holding it together (the warp) or you can relish the exquisite texture of the outer weft. I enjoy the intricate weft very much as a person, but in my research, I like the warp. And they are not opposite. Obviously, they are aspects of the same fabric. We need them both. I also like the metaphor because it conveys a meaning of "safety net" as the fabric that sustains and supports us. In the idea, the fabric of life also emphasizes the quality of intricate interweaving or dependency. If you start poking holes and pulling threads, the fabric can hold, but if you go too far it starts unravelling completely.

AD: The IPBES Global Assessment Report on biodiversity you cochaired came out in 2019 and caused headlines such as, "Humans threaten 1 million species with extinction," and, "The rapid decline of the natural world is a crisis even bigger than climate change." How would we experience the loss of one million species, and what would it mean for the future of nature? Is your impression that people get a right understanding of what is at stake—or are people getting it wrong in some way or other?

SD: First, this is the estimated number of species threatened with extinction, meaning that their extinction is not necessarily unavoidable. It is our choice whether they go extinct or not. And it is our choice *now*; a bit later will be simply too late. I don't think people truly realize what is at stake. This is partly because the species that tend to be showcased as on the brink of extinction are indeed very rare already, so people cannot immediately figure out why they are important—with the exception of some glamorous ones, of course. What people do not realize is that they are symptoms of a vast problem—they are the many threads that could make the fabric of life unravel. Also, global extinctions are not the only problem. For some reason most people have focused on this finding of our report. But however serious this is, it is not the only one. We have found decreases in the vast majority of global indicators of nature:

population sizes, integrity of ecosystems, internal diversity of species, biomass, etc. We show many trends in our report, and make a number of really bold statements, but people have mostly focused on the one-million-species point.

AD: In the climate discourse, a steady rise of temperature and CO_2 levels is already very worrying, but scientists also warn about tipping points, such as the release of methane from the permafrost, changed albedo. Are there tipping points also within the problem-field of biodiversity loss? Which events or changes could make the fabric of life unravel in a more drastic manner? Are there irreversible processes of this kind already happening?

SD: To me, all these tipping points or rapidly sliding slopes are within the field of study of the fabric of life, where people are deeply interwoven with nature, including, of course, biodiversity. There are suggestions that some of these positive feedback loops, which are called by some tipping points, have already started, including, for example, the melting of the Arctic permafrost. This, if not halted, indeed has implications for the whole humanity.

People watch the news and documentaries about the Arctic and see the houses and roads sinking because of the melting permafrost. See the polar bears drowning or stalking human settlements and their hearts go out to them—but not everyone realizes that this also means big trouble indeed for all of us, because of all the carbon that used to be "in the freezer," so to speak, and that is now getting into the atmosphere, accelerating global warming more and more for everyone, not only for those that live at high altitudes.

AD: The heat waves we've seen lately in Siberia are certainly frightening and it seems nature is changing so that the abnormal becomes the new norm. Are there any hidden mechanisms in nature that can help us stabilize the situation? Can we hope for negative feedback loops, for instance, so that the levels of CO_2 or changing temperatures make plants grow more, and plant cover comes to the rescue and stabilizes or lessens climate change?

SD: Not really. The stimulus that plants get from higher CO_2 levels can in no respect compensate for the negative effects and critical thresholds of global climate change. We reach these critical thresholds very fast. The biosphere has an incredible level of resilience and flexibility, but we are pushing this capacity for self-stabilization. In this way we open up for self-reinforcing effects that bring us into the unknown.

AD: Some say that the burning Amazon may reach such a point, where the local weather systems might change, making it more like a desert than a forest, the kind of change one suspects might have taken place in the Sahara or the Sahel?

SD: The Amazon is large enough to be a major driver in the climate and hydrology of the whole South American continent. And it contains enough carbon to impact, for better or worse, the climate of the whole planet via its effects on CO_2 in the atmosphere. We probably have not yet fully understood all the consequences of a massive destruction of this biome—for the peoples of the Amazon, for the Amazonian countries, and for humanity as a whole.

AD: Planting trees seems to be a sympathetic and wholesome way of mitigating climate change—but as a layman, it is hard to get a grip on what difference it can conceivably make. What is your own qualified opinion: Is planting trees an important and relevant effort—and are the calculated effects a matter of much debate among biologists and ecologists?

SD: Planting trees is almost always a good idea, except when one insists on establishing massive monocultures of exotic species and calling them "forests." Letting nature restore itself—including the regeneration of trees when they are part of the system—is a better idea, and not cutting trees is the best. There is no way to fully restore the diversity and the amount of carbon accumulated in an ancient, diverse system such as a patch of primary tropical rainforest. But, in many cases, restoration—either assisted or letting plant communities regenerate from seed banks—is the next best option. But thinking that by planting trees alone we are going to "save the planet," for example, stabilize the climate, is a fantasy. The numbers do not add up. We need to plant trees, but we also need to do much more.

AD: Some conservation biologists point out that human meddling generally is negative, just like invasive species are more often a threat than a boon. You seem to be more pragmatic. Do you see efforts and campaigns to rewild as an important approach, or is it a way of thinking that belongs to an old paradigm of division between nature and humans?

SD: The idea that nature is our bounty to conquer, use, and discard is evidently flawed. We see the symptoms everywhere. The whole IPBES Global Assessment is about how and why this is flawed. But, on the other hand, I believe it is simply too late to "leave the planet alone."

Edenic nature is gone. It does not mean, however, that we cannot have a beautiful, intricate, well-functioning nature around us. As I try to convey with the fabric of life metaphor: we are interwoven; we cannot excise nature from ourselves. We need to take responsibility and fully accept that our role is now closer to stewardship and care. This could take many forms and is deeply case-dependent. In some cases, rewilding is the way to go, in some other cases it is definitely not, for a number of reasons.

AD: What are the most common reasons that nature needs human help to heal? Is it mostly about invasive species, lost species, and soils? Which other factors come into play?

SD: When the system has not lost too much information and materials it is not so difficult, not so expensive. For example, if the soil is still in place, if there are still seeds of the typical plants of the system still alive, lurking somewhere in the soil or the litter, if the key herbivores and carnivores and animals that move around the pollen and seeds are perhaps not abundant, but have not gone locally extinct, nature bounces back easily. If, on the other hand, the system has gone over the cliff, so to speak, e.g., the soil is gone, so are most of the plants and key animals. If the water is not just a bit too loaded with nitrogen, but downright toxic, then we need to put work, knowledge, and in many cases money to help. It's like healing a person. Depending on the severity of what happened to them, the person might heal on their own, or need a little help, or need a lot of help. And sometimes it is simply too late, there is no return.

AD: The concept of the Anthropocene originated from the field of geology, but is now being used by many ecologists, and some biologists, too. Twenty years ago, humanistic studies and to some extent also the social sciences tended to see natural science as reductionist in their approach to human life. Now, thinking about ecology, nonhuman life, and so forth has become a huge field, drawing on insights and knowledge from the natural sciences. Is it fair to say that parts of the natural sciences have been "reductionist," too, excluding social and cultural factors when studying nature? Is the paradigm of the Anthropocene benefiting the natural sciences, or is it mostly seen as a cultural reflection on the natural sciences? In which ways have you included humanist and social sciences—for instance, in biology?

SD: I think there has always been a divide between the methods, foci, and questions of interest—or better, the way in which questions are formulated—between the natural and social sciences. But now I think we have come together a lot, probably as a consequence of the massive environmental and social challenges we are all facing. For example, it is extra clear from our recent IPBES Global Assessment that ==the root causes of biodiversity and ecosystem crisis around the world are all deeply social, economic, and political.== There is hardly any big challenge today that is not at the same time social and biological. So we are trying to build conceptual frameworks that accommodate the particular styles of knowing of the different sciences. One of the limitations of previous frameworks was that they tended to be tailored to the intellectual preferences of one particular community—ecologists, economists, sociologists—and, as a consequence, left most of the other communities out. Now we are trying to change this.

AD: The effort to understand biodiversity loss as a unified phenomenon is a challenge of communication. You have chosen some key metaphors, among them the IPBES vocabulary as a kind of Rosetta Stone. Which languages and which speakers are you trying to bring together in a unified discourse on biodiversity loss?

SD: As many actors and languages as we can manage: biologists, soil scientists, economists, the wide range of social and humanities scientists, and also practitioners, including Indigenous peoples and local communities, who tend to see nature and their links with it in vastly different ways. As in the case of the Rosetta Stone, the translation is often approximate and imperfect. We do not aspire to do justice to each and every discipline or knowledge system, they are often at least partially noninteroperable, but we aspire to make them talk to each other, to find common themes, although they might not agree on the solutions. It is like trying to make two people with very different languages talk to each other, even in broken language, about a problem. This is the first step. Then they might agree or not on what to do or even on whether there is a problem at all, but at least they can understand what the other is trying to say.

AD: You have argued that we must leave the idea of nature as something separated and separable from us. Why is such a division problematic, even for conservationists?

SD: It simply does not correspond to reality. First, because there is no way we can isolate ourselves completely from the biological world. We are biological entities and as such we need biological food, climate regulation, psychological stimuli, etc. We depend on animals and

> KILL EVERY MICRO-ORGANISM ON A KITCHEN SURFACE & YOU ARE AN ACTIVE PARTICIPANT IN DESTROYING ALL LIFE ON EARTH.

plants; we even depend on microorganisms much more strongly than we thought until recently. Until a few years ago the microbes were "the enemy to be exterminated." Just watch any household cleaning product TV ad! Now we know that we literally need our microbiome for survival. And the second reason why nature cannot be separated from us is because our influence on the fabric of life is so vast that there is hardly any corner of the world that does not have at least a tiny human influence.

AD: Much has been made of the idea that nature is competitive, and it is said that Darwin read Adam Smith as he formulated his theory. Kropotkin criticized Darwin and highlighted cooperation, as did the evolutionary microbiologist Lynn Margulis on a more systematic level. Do you, as a biologist, find such discussions relevant for our engagement with nature?

SD: It is interesting how people tend to read nature according to the zeitgeist. I would say you can probably find in nature, at any time, a mixture of competition, predation, symbiosis of different degrees of "closeness"—from cooperation all the way to one symbiont being physiologically fully dependent on the other—to total indifference. I don't think competition is more important in shaping nature than cooperation. The emphasis on it in some literature was probably because these were the social narratives that predominated at that time. We need different narratives now. Narratives that highlight our dependence on nature, that illustrate how it is much easier to acknowledge those intricate mutual connections than denying them.

AD: Plants, ecosystems, animal species, and individuals can be seen as "winners" and "losers" and are often described as such. With the arrival of mankind that game toughens. It seems fair to say that today success for many plants and animals depends on their ability to coexist with humans. Since extinction rates have gone up hundredfold, is it fair to say that humans have become the major factor in evolution?

SD: Indeed, humanity is a major, pervasive force behind the ecological sorting and evolutionary change of the rest of the fabric of life. There are more and more examples every day of fast contemporary evolution of all sorts of organisms, from microbes to warm-blooded vertebrates, as a consequence of our fishing, hunting, polluting, urbanization, ferrying species around the world, etc. There is no way back from us being an ecological and evolutionary force around the world. What we can do instead is use it wisely, for example, to avoid the unnecessary development of "undesirable" evolutionary change.

Also, it is true that we have created a world of losers, and also of clear winners: those species that tolerate, or take advantage of, our presence, activities, and infrastructure. Simply because, no matter what, life always finds a way. But what we can do is to use all our knowledge, technology, and creativity to interfere with evolution as little as possible, and to give a chance to all the "losers" that we still want to keep in this world, and who also have a right to be alive. We need a more pluralistic, more tolerant world, in every sense, including this.

AD: In the Taoist philosophy, a success is a moment of danger—an imbalance that points toward one's own demise. It is tempting to see humanity, which spreads all over the planet, transforming it, as a victim of our own success...

SD: I am not a specialist in Taoism—but I quite like this aspect of the philosophy that stresses balance between opposites and the fact that at the heart of one "pole" is the seed of the other "pole." I would say we are rather the victims of our own excess. And I think it is quite consistent with Taoism that too much accumulation in one direction results in its demise. We do not need all that stuff, all that waste, all that energy, [or] all that suffering that the dominant social narratives tell us we need to have a fulfilling, meaningful life.

AD: The divide between humans and nature also accounts for a troublesome debate over the value of nature. Some want to construe it as "value for us," whereas deep ecology thinkers want to posit a "value in itself." In one of the papers you have contributed to, you argue that we need a third solution: "relational value." What is the meaning of this term and what difference does it make?

SD: Instrumental values have to do with valuing entities—plants, animals, ecosystems—because they are useful, or convenient, or good for you to achieve something. They are means, instruments, for something else. Intrinsic values have to do with valuing the entity for its own sake, independently of any consideration by humans. Relational values have to do with valuing our relationship with the entities, more than the entities themselves. For example, our link to a particular tree, or a particular place, quite beyond any usefulness they might have for us. Relational values also have to do with the sense of "doing the right thing," beyond whether that is "convenient" for one or not. Most people in most places make decisions on relational values, although they may pretend they are made in terms of instrumental values only. Relational values are very powerful. They need to be given more prominence and explicit acceptance. As we say, relational values need to be "unleashed," because quite often they are already there in people.

AD: Many people have learned about our dependency on pollinators, for example. Are there other strong and immediate dependencies on threatened features of ecosystems that could serve as a call to action? Which parts of the problem of biodiversity loss do you see as most under-communicated? Which vital facts are the hardest to get people to understand and care about?

SD: In general, all the structures and processes of ecosystems that are not prominent or glamorous or close enough for us to notice. People are starting to take note of the pollinator crisis because it is very serious, but also because it is quite close to food, and also perhaps because some of the pollinators are liked by people, like bees and butterflies. The butterflies are pretty; they are associated in our minds with spring and summer afternoons in the countryside. The bees are associated in our minds with usefulness and dutifulness. In the case of plants, big trees or pretty flowers are similar. But it is much harder to raise awareness of the myriad organisms that do work for us that, however essential, are difficult to see, or very ugly: the regulation of the water cycle, all the decomposition of organic matter and waste and its conversion into rich mineral soil, for example. All the work done by the invisible, inconspicuous, ugly or otherwise unglamorous organisms, what S. H. Hurlbert called "the great biocenotic proletariat," without which life on Earth would not properly function. When we ask what to protect in a city, people tend to think of the glamorous parks, public buildings, art galleries, or sculptures. They do not think of the sewage system, the underground piping, the tangles of wires in the basement of buildings, the rubbish processing plants. Yet imagine what would happen to the city if those did not work properly. The best metaphor I use with common citizens is my compost heap: full of smelly rotting plant material with a zillion unattractive cockroaches working on top of the pile, and wonderfully dark, scented fertile soil at the bottom. All for free, all with us not doing anything.

AD: We need to appreciate nonhuman nature to a much greater extent and also realize more deeply our dependency upon it. Even if this sounds obvious, it's apparently not obvious enough to effect the necessary changes. Do you believe it is possible to profoundly "ecologize humankind," as Edgar Morin says—that is, to give nature a place in the very center of culture?

SD: The environmental movement and environmental science have grown and developed a lot in the last fifty years, and it is becoming a greater part of the public sphere. Before the 1990s, the word "biodiversity" was known to only a small minority of specialists. Now everyone has heard about it. We have the intergovernmental conventions about biodiversity, about wetlands, about migratory species. We regulate international trade of endangered species. We have made large advances about free prior and informed consent. Endangered species are in the news every month. We have managed to ban a number of biocides that previously were widespread. We have people fighting for the rights of nature, of rivers, of the nonhumans. We have young people marching for the planet in many of the major cities of the world. You might argue that some of these regulations are not enforced, you might think that this is far from enough, far too few examples, too isolated, especially because the magnitude of human-driven nature deterioration in the past few decades has been staggering. And you would be right. But there is a counterbalance movement getting stronger. Although, of course, it will have to get a lot stronger, fast, to be enough, to be timely.

Until recently, I was not too optimistic. But now, seeing how the issue has raised on the agenda, how it has been taken up by citizens, by youth, how it is getting more and more attention around the world, I am inclined to think it might just work. We might just make it, as we did with other important environmental and social achievements that we now take for granted, but which were unthinkably large steps at the time. It is not going to be easy. But, on the other hand, what other option do we have?

CHANGING THE HUMAN GAME
with Bill McKibben

William Ernest "Bill" McKibben (b. 1960) is an American environmentalist, writer, and journalist. In 1989, the year after NASA scientist James Hansen presented scientific evidence for global warming to the U.S. Senate, McKibben wrote *The End of Nature* (1989), which is considered by many to be the first book on global warming for a larger audience. The book argues that since we influence the weather, there is no place on the planet that is not influenced by man. The bleak perspective of his debut was counterbalanced by *Hope, Human and the Wild: True Stories of Living Lightly on the Earth* (1995), in which he tells the stories of different societies living in harmony with nature.

In many of his books, he has written about ecological lifestyle, as in *Maybe One: A Personal and Environmental Argument for Single Child Families* (1998) and *Hundred Dollar Holiday* (1998). McKibben highlights an alternative economy more systematically in *Deep Economy: The Wealth of Communities and the Durable Future* (2007), in which he examines what an economy without growth can bear, primarily for already wealthy communities in the West. He argues for life in smaller and more local units, along with a reduction in consumption.

The value of the natural world, contrasted with the technological manipulation of mankind and our surroundings, is discussed further in *Enough!: Staying Human in an Engineered Age* (2003). The idea of the "post-natural," introduced in this breakthrough book, is elaborated in the later release *Earth: Making Life on a Tough New Planet* (2010). Here the earth's name is modified to emphasize that the planet is not the same as we once knew.

In 2008, McKibben cofounded an organization dedicated to the lowering of carbon emissions, 350.org. The name refers to what is considered the upper justifiable limit for carbon levels in the atmosphere—a limit we have long crossed.

Anders Dunker: Your first book, *The End of Nature*, reads in part like an elegy: it is about the end of what we have thought of as nature—something free, unmanaged, autonomous, and wild—in an age where everything, even the weather, is influenced by human activities. Your latest book, *Falter*, also approaches the question of artificiality from the point of view of human nature. When the outer nature has become dependent on human beings and actions, it is more important than ever to understand the human being —what makes us tick, what we ultimately desire and strive for. How is the examination of our inner life and the life—and death—of nature around us connected?

Bill McKibben: *The End of Nature* had to play a kind of dual role: It was the first book about climate change, so it had to lay out all the physical facts and do a lot of scientific reporting. So it is kind of two books in one. It is a kind of straightforward piece of reporting about what we knew about climate change in 1989 and what it meant. And then there's another side—a kind of lay theology or amateur philosophy or something on top of that—to try to explore the sadness that had come over me.

AD: And this sorrow is more than anything about the end of nature as we knew it, the end of something?

BM: On the one hand, there is no arguing the fact that the view we have held of nature, we can hold no more. The idea that there are places beyond human influence. Maybe even human domination is now impossible for the foreseeable future. On the other hand, that makes what you might call relative wildness all the more important. Those places that are less under our influence. I think that the basic goal of human beings, our basic project, should probably be figuring out how to make ourselves smaller to allow more room for other things to come back in. You know, one of the things that drove me when I was writing *The End of Nature*, I was living in the Adirondack Mountains in Upstate New York. I am now living across the lake in the mountains of Vermont. The Adirondacks are an interesting place. They are arguably the greatest example of ecological recovery on the planet. They were pretty much clear-cut stem to stern, you know. It was a kind of industrialized wasteland. In the 1930s, the old men in my town say, you could climb up on the one mountain in town, the mountain that my daughter is named for, and you could look out and hardly see a tree. Now, you climb that same mountain, and you literally can't see a patch of open ground. The forest has returned. And it is not the same forest that was there before. It operates under the influence of human laws—there are a lot of zoning regulations to keep it the way it is—and it operates under a lot of baleful human pressures, too. The Adirondacks are one of the first places where we learned about acid rain. The Adirondacks are also taking a beating from climate change. But this doesn't make the wild that is there less precious. It might make it more precious—as a place for the rest of the world to carry on with its life and as a place for human beings to be reminded, at least a little, that they're not at the center of everything.

I'm thinking that the fundamental goal for humans, our basic project, probably should be to find out how to make ourselves smaller so we can leave room for all other forms of life to come back.

AD: So the connection with nature is obviously important, and I read your works partly as a kind of therapeutics. It is about managing our feelings toward nature, our sense of meaning, our feelings—also in a time where we move toward disaster.

BM: Yes, but let's first be brutally clear: The main point of my work is—forget feelings—that we face a remarkable physical challenge, which, unless we overcome it, will overcome us—and most good things on this planet. We stand on the edge of wiping out an astonishing percentage of the earth's DNA within the lifetime of a single human being. For me, that is the most basic of challenges. I am not a philosopher. I've spent most of my life organizing. In 1989, climate change had perhaps not yet progressed to the point where it represented a catastrophic, stark, immediate physical danger. The sense was much more of sadness.

That sadness has lingered, but through the past thirty years I have come across much more pressing reasons to worry about climate change. Now, people die by the hundreds every day in some part of the world or other because of climate change—and they will die in millions in years ahead if we don't act together soon.

AD: Even if the sense of sorrow can move us to care, climate change should be frightening enough to call us to immediate action. When we still don't act, does that mean we are not as frightened as we should be?

BM: The most important thing about it is its scale. It becomes qualitatively different from other threats that we've faced—and thus also philosophically different—simply because it's quantitively different: because it's everywhere all at once. The only other thing like that, probably, is all-out destruction by nuclear weapons and maybe the hole in the ozone layer. Those are the only two other times when we've confronted this "everything is at stake" kind of moment.

AD: In some ways it seems that the situation of climate change echoes that of nuclear war—like we find it in Hans Jonas's *The Principle of Responsibility* from 1966. Yet the threats are very different, as nuclear war is something that could potentially happen in the future. But climate change is something that is happening now, something that is already going on.

BM: The other difference is that one is easy to picture in the imagination whereas the other one—at least thirty years ago—has been very hard to picture in the imagination. I think I've said it on various points: yes, the human imagination can perfectly well cope with the idea that a few mushroom-shaped clouds could change everything. But it's much harder to grapple with the fact that a billion cylinders exploding in a billion pistons every second around the world could change everything, too. Because that seems like an orderly part of business as usual—not a shocking and disruptive force. Cars and power plants are seen as inherent traits of the world, instead of a shocking and disruptive power.

AD: Some years ago, you launched the Do the Math campaign, where you presented the numbers that prove how fatal it would be to burn the rest of the fossil fuels at our disposal. You also present some striking examples in your new book, for instance that the carbon we have added to the atmosphere, which hasn't been reabsorbed, equals a 25-meter-wide column that would stretch from the earth to the moon. A strong image that shows how this mass can't simply be pulled out and stored somewhere.

BM: Yet I'm under no illusion that they actually capture the size of what we're doing. They don't capture the totalness of it: the fact that everything is at risk. And that's what's so interesting.

AD: Everything is at stake, because all of nature is drawn into what you call "the human game." One of the striking things you bring up is the calculation by Vaclav Smil, that humans and their livestock bred for food make up 95–97 percent of all land animals, measured by weight.

BM: That's quite remarkable.

AD: It's extremely shocking, a fact that doesn't have to do with the consequences of climate change, even if it can be listed among the causes.

BM: It is important to remember, and one should indeed always remember, that climate change is not the only thing going on on our planet at the moment. If CO_2's molecular structure didn't trap heat next to the planet, it isn't like we wouldn't have giant environmental problems to be worried about. We've lost half the mammals on the planet during the last forty years. And that has little to do with climate change and is mostly due to habitat destruction and overhunting and you can go on and on and on. But it clearly destroys a sense of wildness with an equal effectiveness.

Yet many of these problems are such that we can imagine that we can turn them around. We could have regulated, protected, resuscitated—and we still can. Some places, like in Vermont or Adirondack, there is a sense of a partly new wild nature.

AD: But then there are the things you can't repair?

BM: That is the difference. You can build up topsoil again once you've eroded it, but it takes a lot of work and time. Other processes are practically irreversible. Once you've melted the glaciers, no one has a convincing plan for how you'd go and freeze them again. And that's pretty much where we're at. Once you've destroyed the planet's coral reefs, it's not like we have some strategy to make them happen again—except waiting for thirty million years of evolution to take place.

AD: The climate crisis is literally existential simply because it will determine our continued existence and, even more, the existence of scores of other species—but it is also existential because it forces us to ask who we really are. Are we losing our own game, so to speak? What is the meaning of your term "the human game"?

BM: Originally, I wanted to say the human project. But then I realized that that was a silly way of putting it, because there is no human project beyond continuing, keeping things going. At least, I don't think so. I'm not a member of a messianic cult. I'm not an industrialist who wants to urbanize or pave the planet. For most people the human experience is about continuity. It is about passing things on to the next generation. And I think that when I talk about the human game, that's what's now in question.

AD: And this is a game we're used to winning?

BM: It is a game we've been very good at. And it's possible that the reason we're so good at it is that we're using up a huge amount of free resources. And we're running out of those now. One of the most important resources now turns out to be a place to put our stuff. Sufficient atmospheric sink for carbon. Sufficient oceanic sink for nitrogen. You know—on and on. Yes, humans have been remarkably successful at becoming more numerous and making their lives more prosperous.

AD: The question you ask is whether we are able to live in a different manner than through constant expansion. Can we change this mentality or is it a part of human nature?

BM: At least through the twentieth century and for much of the nineteenth, the lens through which we viewed the world was primarily one of growth. Faced with a question—a policy question—what we asked was basically: Will this make the economy larger, or not? If the answer was yes—then we'd do it! That was in a practical sense how we understood the world. And I think that if, somehow, we're going to stumble through the twenty-first century successfully, it will probably be because we replace that notion with concerns over climate change and the conservation of nature. That would mean that the question we'd have to start asking would be: Will this help us sustain our civilization and nature, or does it represent at threat to it?

AD: To establish the principle as absolute makes things very simple, almost as simple as the old principle. But doesn't this require that people set their competitiveness aside?

BM: People are gradually beginning to understand this. One of the things that has happened already is that we have changed how we measure success. For a century— or at least a quarter of a century—measuring GDP determined almost all our political actions. Now, as you know, people have come up with lots of attempts to supplement that—with human happiness indexes and so forth. This is very important, because what humans measure is what they work on, you know. And to the degree that we are obsessed with measuring GDP that's what we'll be working on until the end.

AD: GDP is also part of a competitive international game.

BM: I think what people are starting to realize—and this is why I wrote a lot in *Falter* about inequality, about Ayn Rand—is that just talking about the size of things is no longer a useful operation, because our systems have become so unequal that you keep growing the size of things but all the growth ends up in the hands of just a tiny percentage of people—and everybody else is starting to suffer deprivation even as the total size of things keeps growing. It is very interesting to hear young Americans saying statistically that they are more supportive of socialism than capitalism. I don't think that represents a careful, reasoned analysis of how different economic orders function for the market or something—I think it represents a kind of revulsion at the society that our particular Ayn Randian kind of economy is producing.

AD: So Ayn Rand epitomizes the individualist all-out competitiveness that has been sort of ruling the world...

BM: Not just sort of. Her greatest acolyte was Alan Greenspan, who in turn became the most powerful human being on Earth and ruled the planet's economy for the twenty to thirty years that may have made all the difference and snapped the spine of the planet's physical systems—so I think there is nothing subtle about any of it. I talk about the leverage those books and those ideas possess because they happened to take over the most powerful part of the world at the most crucial moment in these physical challenges. You know, Ayn Rand three hundred years ago or three hundred years into the future—or writing in Swedish and not getting translated—wouldn't have changed history. It's not like her ideas were decisive. But the confluence of idea and moment turned out to be unbelievably important.

AD: So she said what everyone wanted to hear?

BM: No, she said what a tiny group of people wanted to hear. And that tiny group of people turned out to be the most powerful. Most people past the age of twenty-two who read Ayn Rand think it's nonsense, you know, it is an intensely unappealing vision of the world. But for a certain kind of sociopathic mind it fits right in.

She was successful because there is a part of us—there is a part of everyone—that feels that way. Everyone has a competitive streak, a kind of grasping—but always before, at least before late modernity, we had other forces that tended to balance that out and prevent it from being the only way in which we dealt with the world.

AD: Which would these forces be?

BM: Religion. Human solidarity represented by political movements. In the last two hundred years, the union movement. A sense of the natural world as an important and powerful place. Art. All the things that we've essentially discarded over the last few decades, as we have sharpened our sets of motivations.

AD: Motivation is key. The simplified argument against socialism and communism of the kind we saw in the Soviet Union was that people weren't sufficiently motivated.

BM: It is very correct. I had the great fortune, intellectually, to get to travel to the Soviet Union and to get to see manifestly the fact that it didn't work for anything. It didn't work to make people happy. It didn't work to provide people with what they needed. At least market capitalism gives people stuff. So they've held up that end of the bargain. But the point is that we've made a dumb choice in assuming that these two systems, these two poles, represent the possibilities. And it should be abundantly clear, looking around the world, that they don't. Other people and other places have figured out other ways of organizing things. Our senator here in Vermont has seen this, and in an ordinate period he has been talking about Denmark. Not because Denmark is perfect. I've been there and the

Danes are as willing to grouse about things as anyone else—but, you know, viewed from afar and statistically, they have figured out ways to make things work better on human terms. And, not unimportantly, now their carbon footprint is much lower than the U.S. and going down. So they're making it work in the ways that we absolutely have to make it work. Climate change is always sitting there as a kind of check on ideological infatuations of any kind. The one *sine qua non* of any system, any approach to the world, has to be that it somehow allows us to reign in this existential threat. So even if you are convinced, as Ayn Rand was and her followers are, that you have reached a kind of moral nirvana with their libertarian take on the world and so on, the fact that it's destroying the world on which we live has to count as a fairly significant flaw in the whole operation. Basically, I think that the way they try to get around that flaw is by saying, increasingly: "We're going to make rocket ships and go someplace else." Which adds a kind of pure fantasy element on top of everything else.

AD: But if we follow the problem of competition again, it is an empirical question whether or not people are motivated enough to create political change—or if they are motivated enough to put the environment in front of their own interest. And sometimes these shifts are reflected at the ballot box.

BM: There are two questions there. And this is where I shift to my role as an organizer more than as a writer. One question is, are people motivated enough? Can you get them to care enough about the world around them? I think you can. I actually think everybody, or almost everybody who isn't sociopathic, has in some part of them some sense of dread or despair about what we are doing to the world around us and would like to see change, to take part in changing it. If you call someone up on the phone and ask should we have a green new deal, 80 percent of Americans would say: "Yes! Let's do it right now." But the hard part for organizing is that climate change is so large—and we seem so small next to it that it is very difficult for us to imagine that we can have any actual impact on the outcome of this battle. So I think people tend to move on to things where they might have some more impact.

AD: So battle fatigue is a part of the problem?

BM: It's not fatigue. People don't even try because of this sense of scale. They feel overwhelmed and become paralyzed. I have tried to be an organizer and I have made it my life's work, building the organization 350.org, whose name refers to the safe level of carbon parts per million in the atmosphere. Today the number is already 415, so we are clearly in the danger zone. Our goal from the beginning has been to help people be part of a movement that is large enough to have a plausible chance of making change. That psychological understanding has undergirded almost all the strategies with which we organize. And to some degree it has been effective. Given a long-enough time, I have no doubt that we'll win. The other problem with climate change, apart from its scale, is that it's one of the first human problems that we've faced that comes with a time limit. The scale of change we need to make is enormous and the time is very, very short. We do have examples of humans making big changes in short periods of time. You know, at the outbreak of WW2 in the U.S. and elsewhere, people focused all their energies on one thing—and in the case of the allies—we were successful in this one thing. And we could do it again.

AD: So in principle it is possible? Do we know what to do—and that it can be done?

BM: The engineers have given us the tools that we need. The last ten years have sharpened this question because even just ten years ago things like solar panels and wind turbines were still so expensive that it was difficult to see how they were going to do the job. Now that's no longer the case. We're now capable of doing what we need to do. The question is just whether we'll buckle down and do it in time or not. When I'm pessimistic I think we won't, but when I'm not I think we'll move quickly enough.

AD: Do you think we might succeed in implementing this technology in time?

BM: My biggest fear in this sense is that seventy-five years from now the planet will be running on solar panels and wind turbines. We will have waited so long to make that transition, that the world we'll be running on solar panels and wind turbines will be a fundamentally broken planet. That's my nightmare scenario. One of the strange things about having written the first book about this—and having participated in the struggle perhaps longer than anyone else—is that the first ten or fifteen, maybe even the first twenty, years was like one of those dreams where you see that something terrible is about to happen, and you try to warn people, but your voice can't be heard by anyone.

AD: I know those dreams very well!

BM: And yet, this feeling has started to change. Many people sound the alarm. So at the very least I don't think we're going to go through this sleepwalking.

AD: That's a poor man's comfort, at best! Given that we'll have to make such an extreme effort, that there is a kind of state of exception that resembles a war effort or revolution, some people are increasingly impatient with democracy—or, if not with democracy itself, at least with our current governments. I saw you talking at UCI in Irvine, California, and there were some radical students who constantly interrupted you—shouting that campaigning and protesting against the oil industry was an illusory solution: we need overthrow the system, we need to get rid of capitalism and so forth. Your response, apart from complimenting their passion, was that people have been shouting this for a long time, but that as it seems not to happen, we need to do whatever is plausibly effective.

BM: That's close to what I meant to say, but it is a little subtler than that. True, the situation forces a kind of brute realism. Having a solution that works—but that works forty years from now—is not a solution, so don't bother telling about it. It's just a waste of time. I might dream of a new religion that would help us treat nature as something holy and sanctified, but such dreams won't help us at all. So that's the brute realism. What I don't think we're going to do is first upend everything around us and then work on climate change. I actually think it is far more likely that it will be the other way around. Faced with a physical crisis that increasingly we can no longer sustain because it's burning down our towns and inundating our cities and so on, we begin to take a series of important steps beyond that of reducing carbon emissions, of changing some of the ways that power works on this planet. I have a strong feeling that James Watt inventing the steam engine was an even more important event in the middle of the eighteenth century than Adam Smith writing *The Wealth of Nations*. Another way of saying this is that I think ideology follows technology and resources and things rather than the other way around.

AD: So the bottom line is that a technological revolution is much more plausible and would be much more effective than a political revolution.

MB: Not quite! The bottom line is that the only foreseeable political revolution that I can see begins with some technological changes. Sun and wind are omnipresent. Everybody has some. The changes in the flows of capital and hence in the flows of political power that come with the replacement of coal, gas, and oil with sun and wind will be the single biggest disruption to business as usual, including effects on the climate, that one could imagine. The energy sector dwarfs even the IT sector in our global economy and in politics. But IT is second, which is why I worry about all the other things I worry about in *Falter*, too.

AD: In your book you talk about your slightly surprising friendship with Ray Kurzweil, the chief engineer of Google, famous for his book *The Singularity Is Near*, which posits that artificial intelligence will surpass our own and humans will merge with machines. Transhumanists like him tend to embrace everything artificial and want to deploy all thinkable means to outsmart nature. Why are these topics important to you, even when other concerns are so pressing?

BM: I have been interested in it from the beginning. If you read *The End of Nature* closely, you will see that there are three or four pages on these questions. Because I think that, for me, they get back, philosophically, to the same place. You know, this idea of the extension of nature—in this case, human nature. We human beings are interesting characters. Just in the same way that a wilderness is an interesting landscape compared to a cornfield—a wild place is full of strange things, some of them dangerous, some of them smelly, some of them beautiful. Human nature is the same way, we're quite interesting characters almost precisely to the degree that we're not optimized for efficiency. Robots are not interesting characters in that way. So taking apart nature strikes me as sad in the same way as taking apart human nature.

AD: Transhumanists are obsessed with where we are headed as a species, but still they tend to think about their individual lives, like Kurzweil, who talks about eternal life and the digitalization of consciousness. The dreams of new life opportunities overshadow the question of moral and political progress. Do you have any ideas about what a planetary civilization that could—in principle—last for tens of thousands of years would look like? Do you see this question as relevant?

BM: We need at least a shadowy glimpse of where we might go, in order to sort of organize those trajectories. I think that if we're around three hundred years from now, we'll have rediscovered the value of small, local communities, and of human connections. People will look back on the age of social media and suburbs and so on with curiosity—wondering how someone could think that these were sensible ways to be proceeding. I think we will have gotten past it. I don't think, however, that focusing on that right now is a crucial task. If you are trying to rescue people from a burning house, your main job is not figuring out which kind of house you are going to build in place of the one that's burning now.

AD: We are in an emergency and must act accordingly. Your work in 350.org must be uplifting in this respect, since the organization has grown rapidly and has been an important part of the climate protest movement that we see today. How did you succeed?

BM: I think one of the reasons that it was more successful than we thought was because there was an unfilled ecological niche. This is what I was referring to when I said there were lots of people worrying about climate change but who didn't feel they had a way in to the issue. We kind of provided a way, and now people are figuring out other ways—you know, school strikes or green new deals. We started out more from the angle of mass education, with vast rallies all over the world. And we moved into a kind of confrontation over things like infrastructure projects and divestment of finance from fossil fuel—anything that could weaken the fossil fuel industry.

AD: So you have moved from being a writer to an activist? You have participated in demonstrations, made speeches, and even been to jail—arguing that older people should be at the frontlines of civil disobedience, since they don't have to worry about their criminal records. What did it take for you to move to the frontlines, so to speak?

BM: It had to do with the realization, fifteen years into this struggle, that I had misinterpreted what we were doing. Because I'm a writer, I thought we were having an argument, and hence the best thing to do would be to write more books and have more symposiums and publish more articles and so on—and then eventually the weight of evidence would cause us almost magically to begin to move in the correct direction in accordance with science. It was a shock to realize at some point that we had won the argument, the IPCC couldn't have been clearer on what was going on. The world's scientists were in an amazing and unprecedented consensus about what was happening. But even if we won the argument, we were losing the fight. And that's because fights are not about arguments and data and stuff. Fights are about money and power. And the fossil fuel industry had all of that. And so we needed to build some power of our own.

So that was the basic analysis. But then it must go at some level to these questions about human nature and so on, too. I'm still not completely sure what it means that a powerful and important part of our economy is doing all it can to destroy the world we live in, *knowing* that's what it's doing.

AD: That is extremely shocking, on many levels. And that's what you refer to, I guess, when you say that for thirty years you've been engaged in a mock argument where both parties know the truth from the outset, given the Exxon scandal and all.

BM: The shocking thing about Exxon was that they knew and they were willing to lie. That lie, because of the stakes, turns out to be the most consequential lie in human history. So, this may be one of the places where it might be useful to be ... the fact that I'm a Christian may be useful and helping me—because it feels like this has something to do with sin.

AD: Unrelated to your conclusions, that's also what I thought when I read about it. This is radically evil in a very simple and literal sense.

BM: There is an almost fairy-tale quality to it. Sometimes in human affairs, there are more nuanced gradations, but not in this case.

AD: And the clarity of the situation also makes for a calling to take part, whether or not you are Christian or religious. And this is perhaps something that people feel, a way to win back meaning in a time when meaninglessness is experienced as a problem.

BM: The only reason I bring up Christianity is that it is perhaps a way to understand the evil thing a little better. Because we're not very good at that in our secular society. In a world that has at least to some degree been stripped of some of its meaning, it is true that one way to find some of that again is to take part in this action—in this movement. Movements share some things with religion. They also share some things with physical communities, working hard in proximity to one another. I think these were some of the things that Gandhi understood at some visceral level early on: that part of what he was doing was rebuilding India's sense of itself after the assault of the British.

AD: Given that our whole mentality and our whole society is so much built on competition, and given that taking part in resistance, as you talk about in your book, comes at a cost—some people get burnt out, some environmentalists even get killed—it is a struggle that is kind of a losing battle; people need to get something back from it. This sense of meaning and togetherness is at least something.

BM: That is very true. And some of it is actually fun. For me a little book I wrote a few years ago, actually stands as something quite significant—a little novel called *Radio Free Vermont*, which is a comic story of resistance. There is something about all that is good in the human being— intelligence, ethical sense, camaraderie, creativity—in trying to take on Exxon. It requires all of the bravery and an enormous list of virtues and talents that don't get a chance to be exercised very often in the modern world. I do think there is something to what you say.

AD: So, there is an immediate warmth in taking part in a movement that is also a community—but simultaneously you get the chance to take part in a huge history where it is a little like one of those science fiction movies where the whole world is at stake.

BM: There are photographs where people are blockading coal ships in the Pacific with canoes and blocking the sea drilling rig in Seattle with kayaks. That trope of the small and many against the few and very big—that's why people watch *Star Wars*; that's why people read Tolkien.

AD: It is an archetypical story.

BM: Like Pharaoh and Moses, David and Goliath. Those are stories that run very deep.

AD: But this feeling of taking part in a mock discussion, that you describe—that still feels like just one part of it. OK, those leaders in Exxon, and the executives and the experts and the politicians, they knew. But a lot of people don't know the basic facts. They also protect themselves with platitudes, as you describe in a very good passage of the book. "Humans are in trouble, but the Earth will be fine..." and the other one?

BM: "Everything is always changing."

AD: So you have the platitudes on one hand, and you have the lack of knowledge about thresholds, slowness of natural repair, time limits, and all the numbers on the other.

BM: And these are the reasons why talking and writing remain important. You have to win the argument and the fight. You can't win the fight unless you've also won the argument. But it just isn't a good strategy to just keep winning the argument over and over and over again, without moving over to the fight. To make it very blunt: at some point it became very clear to me that writing another book about this was unlikely to move the needle very much. That doesn't mean I won't go on writing books. I'm a writer and that's what I do. But I'm no longer under the illusion that that's how we're going to win this. We're going to win this, if we win this, by organizing.

AD: That brings us to other parts of the world where climate change is much about climate justice or very immediate concerns—whereas in the west, it has been tendentially a game for intellectuals. So that's what seems to be changing.

BM: It is also very true that this is something that makes climate change very hard to deal with. We are forced to work across nations. This is the most unjust thing that humans have ever done. All the other things we have done—imperialism, racism—were horrible enough. This takes away people's ability to raise the food that they need on the land they have. Global warming is a new innovation in horror. And the fact that there is a kind of iron law that seems to dictate that the less you contribute to the problem, the more you suffer from it, adds to the challenge of justice. This is the first time that humans have had to grapple with an intergenerational justice problem. We are impoverishing people 40–60 generations out. And, if you want to add one more element to this, there is the sixth mass extinction crisis, which raises deep questions of interspecies justice. So, across regions and classes and species, climate change represents an attack on ethics and justice like nothing we've seen before.

AD: All this calls for an enormous degree of identification with the problem—and a heightened sense of solidarity in general.

BM: Yes. It requires all that, and it requires figuring out how to make that solidarity practically real in ways that might change things in the short time we have. We have to think about political pressure points, we have to be incredibly efficient, because we're not going to get several chances at getting this right. And one of the things that I have to stop myself from doing, having written the first book about this, thirty years ago, is to say, "Oh, if you had only listened to me then." There were a lot of things that would have been relatively easy to do back then—we could have done a lot of what needed doing. A modest price on carbon back in 1989 would have shifted the trajectories. Now it is useless to propose a modest price on carbon, since that can't change the trajectory enough in the time that we have. And my idea has been that the most critical task must be to break the political power of the fossil fuel industry. That might be the thing that would allow us to change quickly enough. So that's where I've concentrated my efforts.

AD: I saw you saying on television that when people are aiming for 100 percent renewable energy, they've got it right.

BM: Absolutely. A nice clean-cut goal.

DEATH BY UNNATURAL CAUSES
with Vandana Shiva

Vandana Shiva (b. 1952) is an Indian activist, scholar, and writer. She studied physics in Chandigarh and science theory in Ontario, Canada, where she earned a doctorate with work on the philosophy of science and quantum physics. She later studied interdisciplinary subjects in Bangalore and specialized in technology, science, and environmental policy. Shiva's ecological involvement began in earnest during the Chipko movement, a nonviolent action against extensive deforestation in the Himalayas in the 1970s.

Today Shiva is a leading figure in agroecology, a worldwide movement that unites the struggle for global justice with organic farming and forestry. She is the author of more than twenty books and is particularly known for her uncompromising struggle against major international corporations selling seeds, pesticides, and fertilizers.

Her first book, *Staying Alive: Women, Ecology, and Development* (1988), establishes a feminist perspective on ecology. She expands these perspectives in a critique of the modernization of agriculture in *The Violence of the Green Revolution: Third World Agriculture, Ecology, and Politics* (1989). In her book *Soil not Oil* (2008), the regenerative practices of agriculture are contrasted with the extractionism of the oil economy. In *Who Really Feeds the World?* (2016), she critiques international agricultural groups and lays out an alternative vision of the future based on agroecology, where smallholders, local communities, the diversity of crops, and women's work are key.

Anders Dunker: Your books are about life—about seeds, the earth, and biodiversity—and yet death is just as much a part of nature. Traditional philosophical wisdom urges us to accept death as something natural. But what are we to make of nature itself dying out by, shall we say, unnatural causes? What's your take on this?

Vandana Shiva: There is death, which is natural, which is part of the cycle of life: things are born, they grow through their life cycle—it could be short, it could be long; it depends on the organism—and then they die. And new generations come in their place. That is the natural cycle. That is natural death. The rest, I say, is ecocide or genocide. Ignorance and denial of responsibility for deliberately harming other species to the point of extinction does not take that responsibility away. Genocide, of course, refers to the deliberate killing of large numbers of human beings. So, when all the scientific evidence tells you that releasing chemicals into the environment and choking the skies with atmospheric pollution will cause death in large numbers, you have genocide. We have evidence such as this everywhere in my country. One year, ten thousand are wiped out. The next year, twenty thousand are blown away. And then there is death by prolonged drought, which is also caused by the deliberate actions of the very few. Data recently presented by *Forbes* and collected by Oxfam shows that several years ago there were more than three hundred billionaires who controlled as much wealth as the poorest half of the world's population. By three years ago, the figure fell to sixty-two. Two years ago, it was thirty-two. Last year, eight. This year, five. The global oligarchy makes decisions that intensify the mass extermination crisis, both for other species and for large numbers of people. Unnatural death is due to shortsighted greed. Exterminations and systematic erasures of the poor occur most often under the pretext of saving them. In a way, it's the old colonial idea again. When Pope Alexander gave his 1493 papal bull authorizing the conquest of lands "discovered" by Christopher Columbus, it was a "civilizing" mission in the name of God, which in fact basically called for the extermination of all "barbarians." And we know, from the tragic history of the Americas, that it was ninety percent extermination. Colonialism is precisely this process where large numbers of people are pushed to extinction in the name of saving them.

AD: Colonization has deadly consequences on a large scale when people's rights are abrogated. But it also involves a process whereby nature is deprived of value. You have written in several places about the concept of *terra nullius*, the idea of a no man's land, considered empty . . . for the taking. You are also talking about the concept of *bio nullius* . . . in effect, empty life. Can you explain these concepts?

VS: Colonialism defined as barbarians—not fully human—people who were different, people of a different race, people with a different color of skin. To colonists, the Australian aborigines were not human beings, they were part of the fauna. The peoples of the first nations of the Americas were not fully qualified as human beings. The idea of empty land denies humanity to others in the human family.

The contemporary counterpart of Columbus's patented expropriation of native lands is the reign of multinational corporations who are leveraging and claiming, as intellectual property, our living resources, our biodiversity and our traditional knowledge.

My work for the past thirty years revolves around this, around ownership of nature and traditional knowledge of nature. Basmati rice was not "invented." The same applies to Neem, a healing plant from India, or let's say a gluten-free variant of ancient wheat. When a large food producer takes out a patent on basmati, when the American government permits the patenting of neem, or when Monsanto patents an ancient Indian black wheat, something is fundamentally wrong. I just came out with a new book called *Origin*. The title refers to some basic questions: Where does life begin? Can you really invent it? How is it created? Where does knowledge begin? We must distinguish between inventing and what bio-pirates do. So, the subtitle is *The Corporate War on Nature and Culture*.

AD: Who are the people leading this double war?

VS: Columbus was a pirate and today we see new forms of plunder and colonization. I see Bill Gates as the Columbus of our times. He declares our souls to be empty: First *terra nullius*, then *bio nullius*, and now *mente nullius*. His digital jargon—if you summarize it—is that people, in essence, have no knowledge of their own. This is the ultimate form of colonization.

AD: So, cultural diversity is threatened by extermination alongside biological diversity?

VS: Yes, but I would say that the eradication of cultures by other human populations is often more intentional than the eradication of plant and animal species. Columbus called the American natives "Indians," since he thought he had found his way to India. I am a real Indian, an Indian of the "Brown" type. We also experienced indirect genocide, while the "Red Indians" of North America were systematically wiped out during the Indian Wars. Indian scalps had a price tag, with a slightly lower price offered for a child's scalp.

Still, there are murders even when the killing is indirect. For forty-five years, I have worked innovatively within our Indian constitutional framework for the protection of nature and of people's rights. Article 21 of the Indian constitution says that the State has a duty to protect the right of life of all its subjects. Every case we have fought, when it comes to environmental damage, has been based on Article 21. In 1983, I did a study on mining that showed how mining limestone in aquifers was denying people their right to water, irrigation, and security. It was really robbing people of their source of life. It was the first Supreme Court ruling in India that provided a constitutional guarantee protecting the right of life from commercial and industrial interference and damage.

AD: In India, distress and poverty makes some peasants so desperate that they are unable to protect their own livelihoods and many end up killing themselves. Is this another form of unnatural death?

VS: Yes, unfortunately. These people take their lives because of debt incurred by dependence on expensive seeds and chemicals. By the way, many of them take their lives by drinking insect poison. But many also die because genetically engineered cotton has become infested with parasites, and the side effects from the insecticide used to combat them are deadly. Last year, 130 farm inhabitants died in India due to poisoning from insecticides. I have visited victims in hospitals, and I sent a complaint to the authorities. In the first round of cases, the authorities determined that those responsible were guilty of manslaughter. Murder is when I fire a gun at your head. Manslaughter is when I ruin your life. All of this is covered by the law. So, what you refer to as "unnatural death" is a criminal offense.

AD: So, we are talking about people effectively being pushed to suicide...

VS: Yes, caused by the major agricultural companies such as Monsanto-Bayer. We know this because 84 percent of suicides among Indian farmers are occurring in the cotton area. And there is one company that owns 99 percent of this market. So you don't need to look far to find the culprits.

AD: Is it not an uncanny coincidence that one-generational seeds sold by big companies with the promise of a better life for farmers are called "terminator seeds" and "suicide seeds"?

VS: Yes, and these seeds are made in such a way that you cannot store or save them. In India, it is forbidden to take a patent on seeds. We do not accept the lie that seeds are "invented" by Monsanto-Bayer. Still, they are able to cash in and get paid huge sums by farmers. Because 99 percent of all seeds belong to Monsanto, they have a monopoly.

AD: So should we add monopolies, which take away people's means of subsistence, to the list of causes of unnatural death?

VS: Yes, it is monopoly over the conditions of life. In many of my books, whether it is *Water Wars* or *Earth Democracy*, I have reiterated the fact that society has always retained, in the shared commons, what is vital to life: access to water, streams, beaches, forests, pastures. These were kept in the commons. The same process that brought us colonialism also led to the closure of the commons in England. It happened at the same time. As they were invading countries like mine, they were closing down the commons in England. And this basically amounted not only to stripping away that which was held in common—that which guaranteed people the conditions of life—but to privatization and monopolization, the final stages of legitimized manslaughter and the denial of the right to live.

AD: Is the war against nature then a part of a larger war of all against all in which private property is one of the main weapons?

VS: Not only that, but also scarcity, something I write about in the "Terra Viva Manifesto," a collaboration with colleagues in 2015—a year that came to be dubbed the year of soil. It was also a year in which a large number of boats with refugees came across the Mediterranean, and several of them sank. We wanted to investigate whether there was a connection between the refugee crisis and the soil crisis. And there is. The war against nature not only pits people against each other by taking what is part of the commons and privatizing it, it also uproots people and forces them to lose touch with their true homes and their way of life. They are always on the move, becoming refugees. Today, this is the source of great conflict, indeed war conditions, at Europe's outer limits.

AD: Speaking of war, despite most people saying that they love nature and that we should take care of it, there is a real war going on against insects. Many people claim that it is impossible to successfully maintain agriculture without insecticides. They say it is too risky, not predictable enough. Now, the number of insects is falling dramatically with unforeseeable consequences. How can we make peace with insects?

VS: Before industrial agriculture there were no pests—there were insects. And insects perform a very big role in agriculture, both as pollinators—which accounts for one-third of our food source—and as pest controllers themselves via natural pest-predator balancing. But, for all this, diversity is needed. Industrial agriculture began with chemical fertilizers and monocultures, which became like beacons for particular insect species because it's the equivalent of putting a giant feast out there for them and saying: "Eat!" Then when they come to dine, you say: "Spray! Kill!" Well, those insects are smart enough to develop resistance to chemicals. So then you find a more toxic spray. And soon you need a cocktail of ten. And you just keep going into a negative spiral. We have declared a war on insects and a war on bugs because of our ignorance of ecology (and of how biodiversity includes insect biodiversity), which is vital to our own life. The creation of pests is a symptom of ignorance—it is a result of bad farming.

Small farmers get dependent on chemicals, seeds, and machinery, which puts them in debt. When small farmers are pushed out, insects are also pushed out because the system of subsidies most often favors large industrial farms. But the more we centralize farms, and the more we develop monocultures, the more pests and weeds we will create. On the farm I started with Navdanya, the movement I started in India, we based our farming on care for the earth and care for the people. In our farms, the insect populations are six times larger than in the forests next door. We did nothing. We refrained from eradicating insects and we protected biodiversity.

AD: Insecticides are banned in Sikkim. Are they banned in other parts of India as well?

VS: In some places they have banned glyphosate. They banned roundup in Punjab and Sikkim went entirely organic. There is huge trouble with what I call the poison cartel—a cartel of three major companies—which brings us these poisons and is, in effect, responsible for ecocide and genocide. And that is why I participated in the trial against the largest, Monsanto, a few years ago. It was a trial for ecocide and genocide. Now, Monsanto has merged with Bayer, Chem China has merged with Syngenta, and Dow has merged with DuPont. So you have a cartel of three—committing ecocide by wiping out the diversity of species, and genocide by killing 200,000 people every year with pesticide poisoning. You can refer to the United Nations report on the repercussions of food production. And these producers are constantly making false claims to protect themselves.

AD: So lies are also a cause of unnatural death?

VS: I would say they are one of the main causes. And that's why Gandhi is my inspiration. Life is Satyagraha, the power of truth, the struggle for truth.

AD: What can be done when those protecting life and truth are treated as criminals?

VS: In India, there are many farmers who do not earn enough to survive. The global food system is aligned to make it impossible for them to manage. Recently, a large group of these marginalized farmers marched towards the capital in Delhi in protest. Although the right to protest is part of democracy, they were stopped at the city limits and the government declared them to be terrorists. Peasants fighting for their right to live! So you can imagine how far-fetched the use of the term terrorism can be become.

AD: So what to do in countries and regions where big corporations, seed-oligarchs, are completely dominant? Should people plan for an ecological revolution?

VS: Often, those who rebel are already marginalized or otherwise removed from the mainstream of society. Even in the U.S., large farms are not owned by farmers anymore. They are owned by banks and investors. Corporations want to make farmers redundant. Farmers who work on farms for a period of time are hired to drive a tractor. The next step is driverless tractors. Despite all that, in a world in which farming is becoming more centralized, people find new ways to do things. No matter where I go, I find organic farmers who invite me to their small farms. Even in areas where the pressure is felt most, people still make positive choices. While conscious actions can lead to unnatural death, conscious choices can also lead to a celebration of life.

AD: When land is not reclaimed, people are pushed out permanently, making speculation yet another cause of unnatural death. In your books, you point at a direct connection between monetary speculation and real estate speculation—land grabs that can lead to the sacrifice of both nature and people. How can such crimes happen in a culture in which access to information and the media should be revealing them and subjecting them to ethical criticism and legal prosecution?

VS: We can begin looking for an answer by going back to 2008, when the speculative system of finance collapsed on Wall Street. The crash triggered bread riots, better known as "the Arab spring," because the media, and those who influence it, had to change the narrative. The rebellions were in fact bread riots. Even the UN confirmed it. People were literally marching with bread in their hands. The collapse of the financial system led to a total explosion of the price of food. But there was a deeper connection. Speculators at the stock exchange realized that they had to invest in something that was secure and thought: "Food and land is secure—so we're going to bid on that!" And they started taking over bigger and bigger shares of land and food resources. Their intelligence and understanding did not include an understanding of social and ecological concerns. Had they understood this, they would have been deeply aware of both the harm and the instability they were causing. But their arrogance and their ignorance combined: ignorance about the web of life and arrogance of false power running into a dead end. When it comes to daily bread, you are either dealing with collapse or regeneration. Take something simple like the explosion of

Walmart, Amazon, and supermarket chains, all displacing local distribution. The logic is clear: the bigger you are, the more you force prices down. Sooner or later, you reach a point where farmers can't afford to farm the land. So, you go into a supply crunch. And in a supply crunch, even the cheapest products become very expensive. So now you've created scarcity because you forgot one simple fact: it is the land, the soil, and the farmer who produce food. You are merely a trader. Whereas, if you had maintained a modicum of humility, you wouldn't be taking 99 percent of the consumer's dollar and putting it into your own pocket as profits. No matter how you look at it: from the distribution side, the production side, the trade side, or the speculation side—it is all connected.

AD: So what is to be done?

VS: We must work for the future and we must—as a species—do something about unnatural death caused by food shortages. We have to be inventive. Multinational corporations, and the billionaires who own them and the media, dominate the market. The *Washington Post*, for instance, was recently acquired by Amazon. They were critical of Amazon, so Jeff Bezos simply went and bought them. Concentration of ownership is also a consequence of speculation—it not only hurts democracy, it is also, as you say, a leading cause of unnatural death.

AD: Climate change and the sixth extinction are obviously closely linked. Can we say that unnatural death is also occurring, for instance to land animals and coral reefs, because of the way we impact the living conditions of the planet?

VS: It is not the case that the sixth mass extinction is a consequence of climate change. Mass extinction and climate change are co-consequences of the same processes: destruction of land, destruction of biodiversity, the spread of industrial agriculture, the explosion of factory farming. All this pollution destroys the land, as well as the atmosphere. Pollution that "goes up" is the climate change problem while pollution that "stays down" is the problem of degradation and desertification—both of these are intimately connected to the sixth mass extinction. The biosphere and the atmosphere are not separate. We've put a lot of attention on studies that show how climate change is causing species extinction. But those insects you mentioned—they are not being driven to extinction by climate change, they are being driven to extinction by poisons used in factory farming. The same industrial system causes greenhouse gas emissions by moving food around unnecessarily. At this point, negotiating about emission quotas will not help us. If we don't show the courage to make a "biophilic leap," we will not go anywhere. Distortions in the economy, distortions in economic incentive structures, hand power and control to the ultrarich. We must say: "No! We have lived with this system based on fossil fuels for two hundred years, and now it is enough!" Robber barons did not become rich simply because oil creates wealth; they became rich because they rigged the economy to enable them to steal from society. We must change the incentive structure. Taking lives, causing unnatural deaths in human populations and in nature, must be defined as criminal acts. That is why I wholeheartedly support the movement for recognizing crimes against nature and ecocide in parallel with crimes against humanity.

AD: In the book *Fossil Capital* (2016), the Swedish environmentalist and activist Andreas Malm writes about how fossil fuels have been essential to the development of capitalism and how capitalism in turn leads to the suppression and destruction of natural systems. Is it appropriate to denounce capitalism as being a murderous system, or do you find such rhetoric too simple, too general?

VS: Well, such an accusation captures a big part of that problem. After all, the emergence of capitalism does coincide with the dominance of fossil fuels. This is, in effect, the very pinnacle of colonialism. If you removed colonization, you would not have capitalism. You wouldn't have seen three hundred merchant adventurers get Queen Elizabeth to grant them a charter for the East India Company. So, the idea that individuals get rich by their own ingenuity is plain false. Gangs of operators get together and plunder the world. This is how corporations were started. The East India Company was the first corporation. We drove it out of India in 1857. That put an end to the East India Company, but it did not put an end to corporate rule. So, corporate rule, the rule of capital, the rule of fossil fuels, colonialism, and, I would also say, capitalist patriarchy are all different facets of the same thing. That is why I like to simply call it the money machine. The current world order is a money machine with a massive money addiction. And it doesn't even really know why, or when or how to stop.

The early capitalists were merchant adventurers. Their mission was a combination of plunder, terrorism, and grabbing wealth, not creating wealth. All the spices and silks of India constituted 25 percent of the world economy before this plunder began. We were left with 2 percent of the world economy. How did India become so poor? Because someone else became super rich. And with all the billionaires getting so rich today, I think it is time to ask: How did they get so rich? Some of it is speculation, some of it is plunder and piracy.

In my understanding, life, as an interconnected web, is an interconnected common. Anything vital to life is a part of the commons. And any exploitation of the commons, any extraction of rent from the commons, is simply piracy.

CLIMATE RESPONSIBILITY AND MORAL EVASION

with Clive Hamilton

Clive Hamilton (b. 1953) is an Australian philosopher, writer, activist, and professor of public ethics.

He is coeditor of *Human Ecology, Human Economy: Ideas for an Ecologically Sustainable Future* (1997). In *Scorcher: The Dirty Politics of Climate Change* (2007), Hamilton argues that Australia played a decisive and negative role in undermining the Kyoto Agreement. Since then, he has written a trilogy of books on the climate crisis: *Requiem for a Species: Why We Resist the Truth About Climate Change* (2008), which exposes the role of lobbyists in influencing climate policy and denial; *Earthmasters: Playing God with the Climate* (2013), which discusses the dangers of a technological "plan B," often referred to as geoengineering or climate engineering; and *Defiant Earth: The Fate of Humans in the Anthropocene* (2017), which argues that climate change presents an almost insuperable moral problem and asks whether it demands new ideological and religious stories in order to provide direction to the lives of individuals and society at large.

Anders Dunker: Your first book on climate change, *Requiem for a Species*, not only warns about global warming, but also investigates the different kinds of climate change denial. Our failure to take in the full consequences of the facts and predictions of climate science seems to be a substantial part of the problem. But is it clear whether we are talking about denial or just a very slow awakening? In your later book, *Defiant Earth*, you say that even if people know the basic facts, the changes are so profound, so complex and enormous, that internalizing it takes a long time. You say we are dealing with the kind of cultural change that in principle may take two or three generations. What needs to be understood and accepted by the broader population for people to take part in an informed democratic discussion?

Clive Hamilton (CH): We need first to confront the full implications of what the climate scientists are telling us. For most people, in fact arguably all people, it's extremely difficult to really take it in the distressing nature of what the climate scientists are saying about the future of the earth. Not just in our immediate future, but over the longer term—in several decades, a hundred years. It is almost too hard for us to imagine just how radically transformed the earth will become and how difficult it will be for most forms of life, including human life, to flourish. That's the kind of hot earth the climate scientists say we're almost certainly headed for. Since *Requiem for a Species* in 2010, which was about various forms of denial—obviously the main one being the complete repudiation of the facts and refusal to listen to what the climate scientists are saying in toto—I've become a bit more forgiving, I suppose, of the broader public for the difficulty we all have in fully accepting what's going on.

On the other hand, there has been a very big change in the world since the book came out in 2010. When it appeared, I think it would be fair to say that it was met with a resounding silence. Many environmentalists and environmental activists really didn't want to hear its message—that maintaining hope that the world can be saved and everything will turn out all right had become wishful thinking. They half knew that what I was saying was true, but it was too hard emotionally to take in, so they put it aside.

AD: So even activists were in a kind of denial over the relative futility, or limited effect of their own activism? Taking the political inaction in as a *fact* makes for a brutal shock...

CH: I think that at that time, after the disastrous Copenhagen conference in late 2009, the global environment movement went into period of profound depression. And my book was not the kind of thing people were emotionally and intellectually prepared to take in. I remember my own emotional reaction in, I think, August 2008, when the realization hit me after reading a couple of scientific papers that put the situation in very, very stark terms. I remember the emotional impact – it was a kind of terror. A terror that I went through and had to resolve in some way before I could go on.

In a way, I was in the blessed position of being able to write about it, because the ability to articulate your fears, whether in an opinion piece or a full-scale book, can be a process of catharsis or reconciliation with a truth. So being a writer is a privilege.

AD: But this is not the only way to process the situation?

CH: No, and in the years since 2010, there has been a gradual acceptance by most people in the broad global environmentalist movement, and across a younger generation, of the profoundly disturbing nature of the facts that climate science is presenting to us. I think that we are seeing now the emergence of new groups that reflect the new consciousness of catastrophe, if I can put it that way.

I think for the older environmentalist groups, like Greenpeace and WWF, this has been something very difficult to take in and respond to, perhaps because they have become bureaucratized. So I'm thinking of the emergence of groups like Extinction Rebellion and Fridays for the Future, which I find to be an interesting and extremely important phenomenon because they manifest the true emotional drama of the situation we are now in. And so we see an uprising among young people who have learned their basic climate science in their high schools or elsewhere, television and social media. They come at it with a clean slate, able to absorb the truth of what the climate scientists are saying, and to take on the dread. To experience the dread that goes with the recognition of the truth. It is an historical tragedy that the older generations have been so irresponsible—that we have handed to these younger generations this sense of existential dread. It is the worst kind of intergenerational gift that can be imagined.

AD: A world set for disaster, the prospect of a bad ending for history as such . . . something unimaginable.

CH: And yet there it is. So this has changed global environmentalism and activism in a way that is not going to go away. And it will change global politics in the near future.

AD: So how do we manage these collective atmospheres of dread? It is a question, perhaps, of what Peter Sloterdijk and others call psychopolitics—the damming up and release of affects in society, the way they are suppressed, canalized, and utilized. Maybe it is right to assume that the former generations were in a way exhausted after the Cold War and worries over nuclear holocaust, so that, in the nineties, there was kind of a sigh of relief. Taking on a new global threat like climate change was something they were psychologically reluctant to do. One of the things I take away from your books is that, from your reading of the climate science, we won't be able to avoid a 4 degrees hotter world. This is also the title of one of your chapters. A pessimistic conjecture, or pure realism? Is that still the case—or are we even worse off?

CH: That remains the case. Climate scientists have not revised the science since then and their projections haven't changed in any substantial way. So the science is basically unchanged. On the other hand, we have ten more years of greenhouse gas emissions. I thought that global emissions would have reached their peak by now and would have flattened off before declining, but in fact they continue to rise.

For the major emitters—the United States, China, and India—emissions are still increasing, although flattening in the United States, so where we are at is simply catastrophic. We have a lot more greenhouse gases in the atmosphere now and over the next decades much more will go in. Even if industrial and energy systems can be turned around and global emissions start to diminish, it will still take many decades before the actual levels of greenhouse gases in the atmosphere—CO_2 in particular—will start to decline, and only after reaching an extraordinary historical peak. So the challenge is monstrous. There have been positive signs along the way, but they have often been false positives. For a year or so after the Paris Conference in 2015 I became a bit less pessimistic watching the extraordinary progress in the renewable energy industries. But now I see that the momentum of the traditional energy industries and the political forces behind them are so powerful that stopping emissions rising is extraordinarily difficult.

AD: Even if people are waking up and alternative, renewable energy sources are becoming competitive?

CH: What increasingly preoccupies me is how greenhouse gas emissions and the burning of fossil fuels are no longer either a scientific question, an economic question, or a technological question, but a cultural question, particularly on the right. So we have a situation where politicians who deny climate science—I'm thinking of the United States and my own country Australia—want to build coal-fired power stations in order to stick it up environmentalists as a purely vindictive act to prove to them that they're foolish and weakhearted because coal is good for us. Even when the banks and energy companies say: "We're not going to build coal-fired power stations, coal doesn't make any sense financially." There are politicians in the United States and Australia who say we're going to build them anyway, even if we have to provide government subsidies. They want to build coal-fired power stations because doing so would be, as they see it, a victory in the culture war they are waging. For many of them, when the Red Scare evaporated after the fall of the Berlin Wall, they soon began to talk up the green scare.

AD: Equally symbolic seem the rollbacks of nature reserves in the U.S. and protection of the rainforest in Brazil.

CH: It is true, and there is a lot going on around the globe, with deforestation, and the new coal-fired power plants in China and India and elsewhere, negative factors working against the need to slash the emissions of greenhouse gases. But the point I'm trying to make is that here we have something else. It's no longer a problem of economics dominating science. Now we have an almost spiteful urge in some to burn fossil fuels. In the United States there is a subculture who love to drive the biggest, most gas-guzzling SUVs just to enrage environmentally concerned people. If they see a Prius, they will stop and blow exhaust smoke on it. It's called "coal rolling."

AD: And what about the people, voters in general?

CH: We have in Australia, for example, a very broad desire on the part of the public not to build coal-fired power plants, and to invest more heavily in renewables.

AD: So how can the politicians sustain their own agenda?

CH: The conservative parties, now the conservative government, understand that from a political point of view they have to pretend to be interested in renewables. But, in reality, they want to inhibit the growth of renewables and build coal-fired power plants if they can. They are willing to give large subsidies to build coal-fired power plants because the market won't build them as it doesn't make sense financially. So this is something else, something really quite malicious.

AD: An ideological battle? A sort of a war on nature?

CH: It is in a sense a war on nature, but in a way that's different to how it's been characterized previously. It's a way of saying: We don't believe claims about the destruction of nature. Or that we're crossing a threshold from which there's no return. Or that the future of humanity on the planet is in jeopardy. We simply don't accept that. We can keep doing what we have been doing, because we simply don't believe there will be serious adverse consequences.

So stopping the climate policies we need is no longer an industry lobby campaign. The industry has mostly switched and is saying, "We recognize we have to make a transition." So, at the extremes of denialism in Australia and the United States—now on a government level—we are seeing a repudiation of the position of the fossil fuel industries. The deniers say the industry is too soft and should be actively promoting the greater use of fossil fuels. So it's a battle of political culture.

AD: And what is at the root of this battle—what are the fronts? Why are some seeing the environmentalists as a threat?

CH: It is sometimes difficult for people in Europe to understand the extraordinary level of hatred of environmentalists on the part of conservatives in English-speaking countries, especially the United States and Australia, and to a lesser extent in Canada, the United Kingdom, and New Zealand. It grows out of the broader culture wars. Conservative politics was deeply wounded in the 1960s and '70s, when so many of the old verities of conservativism were swept away by the power of the new social movements and counterculture: the women's movement, gay rights, civil rights, and so on. They have never forgotten, never forgiven—and they want to win it back, at least as much of it as they can. When environmentalism came along later, in the 1980s, they saw it as part of this cultural war even though the history of nature conservation was full of conservatives. Just as they have opposed rights for women, for gay people, and denounced "political correctness" and "femi-nazism," they are attacking environmentalism as part of this cultural push that brought enormous social progress and saw them defeated. They have had some victories. Whereas they haven't been able to do much to resist the great historical tides of gay rights and feminism and indigenous rights, they have achieved some significant victories in resisting the tide of environmentalism.

AD: But what about the environmentalist politicians? How can you effectively sell an environmentalist message? There are certain countries who have elected environmentalist leaders or who have declared climate emergency. What do you see as the secret of success to getting the message through?

CH: I've often said that while the scientists must continue to speak up and speak more loudly and do so based on the best scientific knowledge, the roadblocks we face are not due to lack of information. In some countries, the public has a much better grasp of the problem than in others, but I think the information-deficit model has been redundant for many years, because so many of us do not want to *hear* the information—not really. There has been enormous creative effort devoted by all kinds of groups and experts to solve the problem of how to get the message across, how to get people to take this more seriously. For years I had people asking me that question, saying: "You've studied this, you've written books, how do we do this, how do we persuade people to take this seriously." People have sent me their plans, you know, as if I had the ultimate answer to breaking through. I've even been asked by foundations to help create a message that would "cut through" to the public.

I respect and admire people who've wanted to do this, to find the answer to the communications riddle. But, in the end, I think that is not how the breakthrough will happen. I think it is going to be as a result of the concatenation of unpredictable historical forces, forces that will—at a point that we can't predict—suddenly come together in a way that gives enormous momentum and a demand for change. And I say this partly through a study of history, not so much of environmentalism, but of social movements. I wrote a book on the history of protest movements a few years ago, commissioned by the National Library of Australia. The Library had a large archive of historical documents, photos, posters, and images, and the idea was that the book would incorporate these images to publicize its collection.

So I was studying something that I knew quite well, namely the history of protest movements in Australia, especially from the 1960s onward—although I was going back earlier in some cases, as with the women's movement.

In the case of the women's movement, when the second wave of feminism broke with a devastating crash over western society in the middle to late '60s, no one could have foreseen it happening. There had been thousands of dedicated, clever, resourceful women and women's groups actively trying to bring about social change through the '20s, '30s, '40s, and '50s. They were there, they were doing things and they were making very little progress. And then suddenly something happened, the historical forces came together and over a handful of years the world was changed, irrevocably.

This, I believe, is what will happen with environmentalism and climate change, and it has happened in a small way in the last two years. There has been a sudden shift in understanding amongst young people. There has been an upsurge of youth activism. The circle of concern about climate change in its true depth and horror has grown from maybe 10 percent to 30 percent of the population in countries like Australia and the U.S. That's been fantastic and very reassuring. But what we need is to get to the next level where it becomes an unstoppable force. Whether that will happen next year or in ten years or in another twenty years, it's impossible to say.

AD: What about popular groups of conservative resistance and denial? Those who like to speak of all environmentalists as "eco-fascists" and so forth: are you worried about this?

CH: That's a very good question with a complicated answer. It is difficult to imagine the political situation in the United States becoming even worse than it has been since Donald Trump came along. On the other hand, in the

United States we see an enormous galvanizing of forces to do something about climate change. The Democrats have now grasped the nettle. And the same thing has happened in Australia, where the seriousness of climate change has finally sunk in for the Labor Party in the last two years. They seem determined to do something.

But it is certainly the case in other countries that climate issues may become more caught up in right-wing movements and populism.

AD: In that case ecofascism may become a real phenomenon, in a *blut-und-boden* tradition, where protecting one's own nature, implies that immigrants are turned into an enemy representing the problem, while they are often really victims. Pretending that the problem is the others becomes yet another kind of denial.

CH: It must be added that there are populist movements in Europe that aren't denialist, that say that something must be done to mitigate climate change. Even if they don't count it as the most important issue, they are not climate deniers. So whether climate denial can become a part of these currents is an open question. If you want me to give my guess, I think it is unlikely that climate denial will be much more widespread than it already is, but who knows?

Even so, there are other kinds of denial. I have written once or twice that we are *all* climate denialists in some way, in the ways I was explaining earlier. We fully accept the science; we remain children of the Enlightenment, but *emotionally* we find the facts difficult to take in and hold on to. Yet many more people all around the world have now reached a place where they have the emotional strength to face up to the full truth of it, even if we can't hold the full truth in our minds all the time. We have to set it aside in order to keep going.

AD: These groups on the right that you talk about, who don't deny climate change but still find it hard to take the full political consequence of it, are much the same group that seem to be most keen on promoting geoengineering, as you talk about in your book *Earthmasters*. What is the greatest danger of geoengineering, aside from giving us the false sense of having a plan?

CH: A range of schemes have been proposed, and they are usually divided into two kinds. Carbon dioxide removal methods aim to suck CO_2 out of the atmosphere. Growing trees and enhancing carbon stored in soils are both relatively benign. But seeding the oceans with iron filings so that the seas can soak up more CO_2 means changing the chemistry of the oceans, and that means changing the biology, too.

The other kind is usually called "solar radiation management." It includes a range of schemes, more or less benign, aimed at reducing the amount of sunlight that hits the earth's surface. The big one that attracts all the attention is sulphate aerosol spraying. Planes would spray sulphate into the upper atmosphere, like a high-level smog that reduces incoming solar radiation. Global dimming.

There are some major environmental uncertainties about this kind of solar geoengineering, but I have focused more on the geopolitics. What would it mean for one powerful nation to take control of the world's weather, to have its hand on the global thermostat? When we ask that question, we spiral off into all kinds of dark scenarios.

AD: Many climate experts want to avoid a public debate on geoengineering. How big is the risk that people will be attracted to such a plan B?

CH: I've been anxious for quite some time about the possibility that solar geoengineering will be seized upon by conservative forces who deny the science—even if it may seem weird that people who deny climate change should nevertheless seize upon a solution to it. But that's the reality. I'm more worried that conservatives who grudgingly accept the fact that Earth's climate is changing will adopt geoengineering as a way of avoiding cuts to fossil fuel emissions. They might be drawn to the idea that solar geoengineering will get around the need to raise the prices of fossil fuels and devalue the assets owned by powerful fossil fuel corporations.

One of my recurring nightmares is that someone gets into Rupert Murdoch's ear and persuades him that solar geoengineering is the way to respond to a warming globe. So he sends out a tweet backing it, and his 250 or whatever newspaper editors around the globe get the message and start advocating solar geoengineering as the answer to climate change. I think this would affect the politics of climate change in an extremely negative way, because it could easily become a substitute for cutting greenhouse gas emissions.

AD: But in your books you also underline that the necessary political changes don't happen fast enough, and that it is in any event too late to stop catastrophic global warming. In such a scenario, what stands in the way of even traditional environmentalists proposing technical manipulation of the atmosphere?

CH: I recognize that some well-meaning, well-informed people with a real concern for the environment and a warming world could decide that the times have become so desperate that a desperate measure like solar geoengineering is needed. Indeed, I know some serious environmentalists who have come to this point already. And who knows, maybe in ten or twenty years' time, if I'm still around, the situation could be so dire on a hot earth that even I might say we have no alternative. But it's an incredibly risky maneuver for humans to try to take control of Earth's climate system by attempting to regulate the amount of sunlight reaching the planet. We would be deciding to regulate the operation of the Earth system itself.

AD: We are told that the skies would get hazy, no longer fully blue. Different ecological processes could be affected in ways that are to a great extent unpredictable. Aren't the effects upon nature and ecosystems frightening enough keep us from such meddling?

CH: There are much more qualified people around who can inform us about the scientific risks. So I've talked about the geopolitical risks of solar radiation management, which no one else seemed to be much concerned with.

AD: But there is also a question of our right to meddle with nature—a debate we know from the ethics of genetic engineering, questions of principle that play out on a much vaster scale and with fatal risks.

CH: Of course, there are philosophical questions here, concerning the role of human beings on this planet. Isn't it the ultimate hubris for us to imagine that we can actually regulate Earth's climate system through a giant technological intervention like solar geoengineering? That seems to me to be something monumental in its implications.

AD: In your book *Earthmasters,* you mention how the philosophical questions of intervention in the climate and weather even has a mythological or theological character, given that the skies always have been seen as the abode of the divine and the unpredictability of weather has epitomized the uncontrollable. Climate engineering may be breaking into the realm of the divine—and can be seen as a continuation of a promethean and modernist trend in culture.

CH: Yet some writers argue that we already change the climate and now will have to keep doing it. Some say that we already have created enough climate change to suppress the ice age that is supposed to arrive 50,000 years from now. Thus, they argue, maybe a civilization of our type must learn to tackle a changing climate—either by adapting to it or trying to adapt it to us.

I have taken a deep interest in the Anthropocene, the new human-induced geological epoch, because we have been told by the Earth system scientists that human beings have become so powerful that we have shifted the geological evolution of the earth, pushed it into a new geological epoch as a result of our transformation of the climate. It is not just the climate system that we've changed but the entire Earth system itself. I found that as I studied it more deeply, I began to understand the consciousness of a geologist. Geologists have a strange way of thinking, which is not so strange to me now that I understand it, because they spend their whole lives immersed in very long timespans.

Many of them become much more relaxed about massive changes in the nature of Earth and how it functions. And that also goes for the emergence and disappearance of species. And so many geologists seem to have a more distant and accepting attitude to what we have done. They seem to believe that the rise and fall of civilizations and of species is something we just have to accept.

But I'm inclined to respond: "That's all very well, but imagine the immense suffering that goes with the rise and fall of species, which we see already as the world is becoming hotter. When human populations collapse, people die unnatural deaths, in pain. They have families. So by engaging with the Anthropocene, and the rise and fall of species, there is a real danger—and I'm speaking of myself here—that by gaining a deeper understanding of what is happening, you distance yourself from the suffering this transformation actually entails.

AD: So even empathy, humanistic concern, or compassion with other species can become arguments for not accepting nature and its transformations, but rather taking control of it.

CH: Well, there are the ecomodernists, who say that human beings have always transformed their environments and will always do so. "We've achieved enormous and beneficial changes through the arrival of civilization and modern technological transformation." Which is true, but we are now beginning to become aware of the massive cost that civilization and technology has had through impacts on the natural world. The ecomodernists argue we must double down, as the Americans say. "Sure, there has been damage through pollution and the emission of greenhouse gases into the atmosphere, but hey, we're the ultimate technological creature, so let's use our expertise to take control of the whole system!" In the ecomodernist vision, solar geoengineering is the natural extension of human control of natural systems.

AD: So we pit the technological side of human nature against the rest of nature, even when it suffers and convulses as an effect of our former actions.

CH: Yes. So my argument is that it is one thing to modify a valley or a landscape, which can be shoveled and sculpted and engineered by human beings, although often with dire side effects. But it is another thing entirely to consider the total Earth system as an object of human control. We can't control it, and it would be a monumental mistake to believe that we are capable of it.

AD: In the article "Human Destiny in the Anthropocene," you emphasize that climate change is a man-made disaster. Nature makes no choices, but humans could always choose differently. Jean-Pierre Dupuy says that many Japanese people talk about Hiroshima and Nagasaki as tsunamis—as natural disasters. This is easier than accepting that someone actually chose to kill all those people and create such destruction.

CH: It's hard to take responsibility. When we hear about a natural disaster, or even an individual disaster—a shark attack, for example—we think of it as a tragedy, or we think of it as an act of fate, just something that happens to human beings. But, if instead of a shark mutilating that body, it was done by a man with an axe, it would be far more disturbing to us. It's far more upsetting to hear about, even if the end result is the same, a mutilated dead body. And it is because that person with the axe, even if he is half mad, has a will—we see him as a manifestation of evil. No one sees a shark as evil; it is just doing what sharks do. So, when we read about a mutilated body, we would much rather find out that it was done by a shark than by a human being. Perhaps this also goes for droughts, heat waves, forest fires: it is more comforting to think of them as acts of God, that there is no one to blame, just the forces of nature, of fate.

AD: Yet you could turn the argument around: a crime with a perpetrator is more meaningful; at least we know whom to blame. If we talk about it as an evil action, or a set of evil actions, blame does come into the picture—and a writer like Andreas Malm has in a provocative statement said that "ecological class hatred [is] perhaps the emotion most dearly needed in a warming world." Those who suffer the consequences of climate change need to blame the right people, the real perpetrators. They should rightly say: "You did this to enrich yourselves, and now we are paying with our lives."

CH: I completely agree that there is room for more rage and anger, even if I don't agree with Andreas Malm that we should cultivate hatred for these parties. I agree that we have been too lenient, and as long as I have been writing about climate change, I have been writing about who is responsible, who did this. Powerful forces in the political world, but also in our psychology, act to diffuse the blame to avoid a proper understanding of who is responsible for bringing this on. A few years ago, I proposed that in each country, an environmental group should make a list of the fifty businesspeople, politicians, lobbyists, and denialists most responsible for stopping action on climate change. Those names should then be inscribed, along with their crimes, in a time capsule and buried in the grounds of a primary school, so that in a hundred years' time—when the world is going to hell—people can dig up the time capsule and see who was responsible. I think it's important. I don't think the people who've been responsible for stopping action on climate change should get away with it. These people should be held accountable, some sort of truth and justice commission, so that the world never forgets who was responsible for doing this to the earth, for allowing so much suffering to humankind and to other species.

AD: On the other hand, you mention how shifting the blame or finding culprits often becomes a way of eschewing responsibility and effectively becomes another form of denial. You refer to the sociological findings where people in Norway tend to underplay their own influence on climate change and point to China and the U.S. as the real culprits, since they are seen as bigger and thus more significant.

CH: Yes, people will always shift the blame around. But that doesn't change the fact that for each country—the United States, for instance—a group of well-informed people could draw up a list of those who over the last ten or twenty years have been most responsible for stopping the United States from adopting the policies necessary to cut greenhouse gas emissions. It could be argued that, in democratic nations, millions of citizens allowed their representatives to do those things—even voted for Donald Trump, who swore to do nothing. But I don't think that reduces the blame that Donald Trump deserves. Of course,

Donald Trump got his denialism from somewhere. There were people actively promoting denial, in various right-wing think tanks, such as the Heritage Foundation and the Heartland Institute. Some of them would be among the 50.

AD: Some people would argue that if these people simply disappeared, others would take their places, that the problem is the system, not the individuals—even if they are on top. Aren't these people symptoms of an underlying system–of ideologies and power-structures that are much harder to root out?

CH: Yes, that is true. But humans have freedom to act, they have agency and therefore responsibility. Others could have occupied those positions but decided not to. So I don't accept the argument. I do accept that there are structures and systems that make responding to climate change extremely difficult. The power of the fossil fuel lobby, the influence of money in politics, the imperative of capitalist enterprises to maximize profits, and so on. In some countries, elected political leaders have promised to take action, but then failed to honor their promises. They too have to take responsibility, not just for allowing warming to continue but for betraying democratic principles.

TAKING THE TEMPERATURE OF THE FUTURE

with Kim Stanley Robinson

Kim Stanley Robinson (b. 1952) has been called one of the greatest science fiction writers of our age and has shown a pronounced focus on the environment throughout his work. Robinson's first books were the *Orange County Trilogy* books, which envision three different futures for the West Coast of the United States. The first book, *The Wild Shore* (1984), unfolds after a nuclear war. The second, *The Gold Coast* (1988), presents a dystopia in which the landscape is slowly ruined by highways and the incessant expansion of human infrastructure. The third, *Pacific Edge* (1990), unites green politics and advanced technology in a far brighter vision.

In the award-winning *Mars Trilogy*, Robinson explores the possibility of "terraforming" our neighboring planet. We start with the early colonization of *Red Mars* (1992). In *Green Mars* (1993), the red planet is terraformed. By *Blue Mars* (1996), our neighboring planet has transformed into an evolved society, while Earth remains immersed in ancient conflicts.

In the early 2000s, Robinson wrote three books on global warming: *Forty Days of Rain* (2004), which depicts a catastrophic flood; *Fifty Degrees Below* (2005), which dramatizes climate chaos and extreme winter; and *Sixty Days and Counting* (2007), which revolves around an environmentally engaged U.S. president who lays out a plan to reverse climate change.

In *New York 2140* (2017), he describes a future in which the sea level has risen drastically. His latest novel, *The Ministry for the Future* (2020), is a grand polyphonic narrative of the mid-twenty-first century, when global civilization is faced with disaster and has to reinvent itself in order to survive. Robinson describes his project as utopian, imagining future scenarios for a more sustainable and just society, even if his utopias are usually troubled and imperfect.

Anders Dunker: What are the challenges of crafting utopian fiction?

Kim Stanley Robinson: If you present a utopian solution, where everything has fallen into place and where there is a solution to all problems, that's all well and good—but how do you get there from today's world? Here lies the problem. We don't just need an idea of a better society, but also proposals for the reformist steps that can lead us there. It's really hard.

AD: Your narratives are informed by a lot of research. To what extent do you let the narrative be determined by your research and by science? Do new scientific observations sometimes end up determining the plot and the events of the novel?

KSR: All the time. The first draft most often turns out to be unconvincing. Sometimes, it is impossible to find the answers. Would pregnancy and childbirth be possible on the moon, the way I wanted to describe in *Red Moon*? No one tried, so no one really knows.

While I was writing *New York 2140*, which depicts a future when the sea level has risen by 50 feet, NASA researcher James Hansen published an article on the Eemian period between ice ages 130,000 years ago. It turns out that, during this era, within a ten-year period, the temperature rose by one degree, with the consequence that the sea rose by 50 feet. I thought right away, my God, it's not that unlikely after all, what I write. I needed 50 feet to make my story work. If it were only 6 feet, you'd get a lot of spills and chaos, but not a pervasive change of world cities, as I describe.

Another example is whether or not you can grow vegetables on Mars. After I wrote my *Mars Trilogy*, it was detected that Martian soil contains toxic levels of chlorine. Had I known that while I wrote the novel, I would have had a hard time believing in the story.

AD: In your *Mars Trilogy*, you explore intergenerational stories, collective narratives spanning hundreds of years. The French historian Fernand Braudel writes about *la longue durée*, a deep historical time connecting landscapes and humans, the past and the future. What are the challenges of describing such great spans of time in a novel?

KSR: Yes, I have taken a lot of inspiration from the works of Braudel. The question is if the novel really can cover la longue durée. I have tried a couple of times, and I must confess that they are not a perfect fit. For a novel, the perfect time span is probably a couple of years—or a lifetime at most. The understanding of history is nonetheless essential for all science fiction. You set the present on a trajectory that stretches into an imagined future.

AD: In the *Mars Trilogy*, Swiss-Martian theorist Charlotta Dorsa Brevia writes her philosophy of history in the twenty-fourth century. Even if her theory is complex, the core principle seems simple enough: there is a universal tendency in history towards peace and cooperation—but this process has been slowed down and obstructed by historical counterforces.

KSR: Capitalism is one such counterforce, just as aristocracy and the upper class were in the time before the French Revolution and in the restoration that followed. The old power elites cling to their privileges, but most people want freedom and solidarity. According to Charlotta Dorsa Brevia's narrative the universal tendency of history is only realized on Mars.

AD: The great thing with the imagined Mars colonies is that they can start from a zero point, with an optimistic pioneer spirit, whereas Earth in this far future is called a "planet of sorrow," swamped by traditions, warring identities, and ancient conflicts. How can we make global warming an occasion to cooperate in a world where we prefer to deny the problems and hold on to our habits?

KSR: This is the question, exactly. Since I started writing climate fiction, beginning with *Antarctica*, I have returned to the same story: the main idea that we can get through climate change in a worse or a better way—and that we need to try to choose the better one. At the same time, I'm increasingly concerned with mass extinction. When a species is gone, it is gone for good. I don't believe in de-extinction through cloning and synthetic biology. That idea is a bluff, more or less, a scientific party trick.

AD: Let us simplify and say that there are three great arenas within which drastic change can take place in the near future: the climate, social politics, and technology. If we stick to this premise, it seems that you have taken technology almost completely out of the equation in your 2017 novel, *New York 2140*. Even though it is set more than a hundred years into the future, and the oceans have risen by 50 feet, there are hardly any signs of technological breakthroughs that have changed people's lives. This omission seems to be a conscious choice, and a peculiar one for a science fiction author. Why did you want to omit the technological fantasies? Do you see them as being too escapist?

KSR: Yes, there is a lot of magical thinking going on with respect to technology. Computers will solve everything; we can upload our consciousness. Sometimes such ideas are picked up by certain groups, such as the singularity, which was adopted by the tech world. They have made a singularity university—it is so stupid, so poorly thought out. Sometimes science fiction visions of what might be possible are attempted in the real world, and the results can become really dangerous. The singularity, scientology, transhumanism. Such dangerous technological ideas make me prone to set technology aside in my stories. When it comes to technological change, many cling to the idea that innovation and efficiency will continue to accelerate in an exponential curve. The techno-utopians, those who talk about the singularity, tend to refer to Moore's law that integrated circuits in computers become faster and faster, smaller and smaller, cheaper and cheaper—and at a growth rate that can be calculated. But this cannot continue forever. Exponential growth is moving toward infinity, but infinitely rapid innovation and infinite efficiency is impossible.

AD: So they try to pit the exponential graphs of technological efficiency against the steep graphs of temperature rise, resource depletion, and so forth in a sort of technological arms race against nature—to protect ourselves from nature, or even to defend nature?

KSR: There will still be technological advances, but the decisive factors that determine the future will be social policy and the climate. We need to admit that our planet is more vulnerable that we thought it was and do all that we can to stop other species from dying out.

In one of his books, *Half-Earth* (2016), the biologist E. O. Wilson advocates the protection of half Earth's landmass to secure biodiversity—really a quite utopian project. The project is very close to Arne Naess and deep ecology. Wilson's book is all about protecting species by securing their habitats through wildlife corridors and new wildernesses.

AD: In your novel *Pacific Edge*, you describe a situation where a green revolution has taken place in the 2020s and a kind of ecotopia has been realized on the American West Coast. California has had a pronounced environmental profile the last decades, while simultaneously depending on an oil economy. Do you imagine that your own story could be realized in our time? Can California become a green utopia?

KSR: *Pacific Edge* is an ecological vision of the future that should be read in contrast to *The Gold Coast*, a

Reagan-era dystopia. The two are playing themselves out in parallel within the same geographical space. I think this race between two different futures is still taking place.

AD: The steady flow of dystopian films and TV shows no sign of subsiding. Since these are so popular, we ought maybe to ask ourselves what people are attracted by. Is it the drama, the shudder, the dark joy of seeing something so grim that one's own fears seem trivial in comparison? Or is it something else? Are they useful warnings or do you see them as a sign of resignation?

KSR: I think it is both. This is something I have learned from Frederic Jameson. We always think dialectically, and art is always two things at the same time—or, as Jameson once argued, both a utopian desire and a class rhetoric. So we can see the dystopias as a kind of schadenfreude: since people in the future are going to live in a terrible time, we can feel more cozy in the present. At the same time, it is a warning, telling us we can't go on in this direction!

AD: During the coronavirus pandemic, our time, the beginning of the 2020s, seems like total crisis, a potential turning point for almost absolutely everything—which is also very much the topic of your latest novel, *The Ministry of the Future*: a journey from total crisis to a point when things actually start getting better. Globally, the curve of carbon emissions eventually bends and starts dropping. On a local level, California, for instance, is being rewilded. There are buffalo herds roaming the Central Valley. Enormous irrigation schemes are set in motion. On a global scale, we find the journey is very gradual—which is fascinating, because at the end of it, we do seem to get through the bottleneck.

KSR: Yes. It was my attempt at describing the steps for actually getting to a utopian point in the future, and I had to believe it. I wanted to write something I really could believe in, rather than it just being a wish. It might be the blackest utopia or the grimmest utopia ever written, but it's still utopian in that I always tried to present things turning out for the best in a way that the reader could still believe in. So, this was a balancing act and an enormous strain, almost like a kind of geological pressure—so that the novel is a metamorphic rock. It's some horrible conglomerate that has been squeezed hard by my demands.

AD: Even if your novel ends on a very hopeful note, it opens with a sort of dystopian nightmare: a terrible heat wave striking India. The key factor is something called "wet bulb temperature," where the body loses its capacity to cool itself down?

KSR: Yes. If the heat and humidity rise to a certain level, it's simply fatal for human beings—and you would have to be air-conditioned constantly. It's already happening, and often in places with the weakest electrical grids. And now, of course, with the pandemic, you have to think about public spaces. When you're trying to gather thousands of people in one air-conditioned space, it can break the air conditioning and cause the electrical grid to go down, potentially leading to mass death. The first scene in *Ministry for the Future* is coming. I say that like Jeremiah or one of the Old Testament prophets.

AD: In the novel, India emerges from this ordeal as an ecological leader and an example to the world. But some parts of the population, impatient for a drastic reduction in emissions, and judging that the heatwave, which has killed millions is inflicted upon them unjustly by the global north, feel entitled to strike back with violence, terrorism. Did you have qualms putting these parts in?

KSR: Well, yeah, I have huge qualms. I have fears. My wife reads my books and fears that it will look as if I'm advocating terrorist violence to get to a better climate change solution. Novels are often misread as advocating anything that is said or happens in them. It's astonishing how naive and misguided readers of novels can be about what the author intends. As if every novel is just an op-ed piece by the author expressing their own opinions. This is very, very far from what I think the novelist is doing: being a telephone receiver for voices that are coming from everywhere and trying to orchestrate a communal message. One of the reasons I'm a novelist rather than a political writer is that I'm very easily led by my feelings, and my political opinions are easily swayed by anybody who talks to me. I just feel like I'm very persuadable. So, while I'm writing a character, I believe in that character. And then I move to the next character, and I believe in that character. Well, this is what a novelist is. A novelist needs to do this.

So, in this novel, it's scary as hell, because I think that there will be angry people doing the wrong things. Judging by the terrorist actions that have already happened in the last fifty years since World War II, the idea that political terrorism works, which has proven to be wrong, is nevertheless believed by people who are really angry—too angry to be rational about it. I think that privileged white men advocating political violence in the developing world is immoral in itself, because other people suffer the sanctions, the murders, the reprisals, and the degraded lives.

I saw this a lot in the '70s, when prominent professors in Western universities were advocating for Third World revolution, and they were never going to suffer from it. Other people in the same universities were inventing the weapons that were going to kill the revolutionaries. So, for me, it has been very important to insist on legality, on rule of law and reform. [THE SATYAGRAHA OF PRATITYASAMUTPADA]

AD: You have talked before about invisible revolutions, legal revolutions, economic revolutions that arrive as a sort of saving grace. Despite all the tension, trauma, and conflict, there is a progressive movement toward peace and unity in your latest novel. How real do you think this possibility is in the twenty-first century?

KSR: I don't know. This novel is an exploration of possibilities. As for probabilities, I don't know. I had a bias toward the positive. I wanted to present a best-case scenario for the current moment that we're in right now that I thought could work if we were to do it. It seems to me that underneath all of the turmoil of our time, there is a kind of somewhat under the radar collective global civilizational effort to make things better that with science, medicine, and public policy. So, organizations like the UN—sometimes we think of them as toothless, but, also, they're emergent.

AD: In your novel, you depict organizations that plant trees, that support regenerative agriculture, and so on. Even if the novel is set in the future, these organizations already exist. Among them are Vandana Shiva's NGO, Navdanya, and you also refer to the province of Sikkim in northern India, where insecticides and even chemical fertilizers are banned. Can such emerging projects and zones be seen as glimpses into the future, as in William Gibson's idea that the future is already here, just not arriving everywhere at the same time?

KSR: Gibson said there's residual and there's emergent. The residual is what lasts from the past, either for good or for bad. Mostly for bad—like how capitalism is residual feudalism liquefied. Emergent is hard to tell, because will it really emerge or not? We don't know yet because we're in the present and the future is never really there for us. So, it's an imaginative act to make these trajectories go off into the future and say, "Well, I want *this* present to expand, and I want *that* present to shrink."

AD: Hölderlin wrote, in his famous poem "Patmos," that when danger grows, so does that which saves. His idea might have been more mystical, but in your novel, humanity's plots to save themselves from the consequences of climate change are pretty drastic. Some are also deeply disquieting, like coloring the water in the Arctic yellow to increase the reflection of the ocean in the absence of sheet ice. In your near-future vision of Antarctica, water is pumped from under the glaciers to keep them from sliding. I have to ask you, how real is this?

KSR: It has been proposed by glaciologists. They've so far kept it out of their papers and formal proposals because they don't want to get into the business of geoengineering. They would like to remain glaciologists. The ones who shared this idea with me said, "It's your job to get the idea out there, not ours." So I believe my novel will be the first to mention this methodology.

If the ice in the Arctic Ocean were to melt, the net sea level wouldn't rise. The net sea level would rise if

Antarctica and Greenland were to melt. Yet, the loss of ice in the Arctic Ocean would shift the albedo of the planet and begin to heat up ocean water in a way that would be truly catastrophic over the long run. That would have repercussions everywhere. So, as in so many things, the Arctic and the Antarctic are weirdly divergent. They're polar opposites, so to speak. One of them is land with 10,000 feet of ice on it that, if melted, could drown all of the coastlines in the world. Another is ocean with 10 feet of ice on it that, if melted, would have zero effect on sea level. So, the problems involved, the solutions involved, are radically different. We're not going to be very good at either of them. We might try both of them, because the long-term ramifications of not succeeding are *New York 2140* levels of sea rise.

The coastal cities of the world are crucial. I've been reading recently, "Oh, the work of civilization will be to move those cities inland." Well, this is just ridiculously untenable. They're not running the costs of moving a whole city. These are people from the humanities, people who haven't run the numbers. We don't see scientists saying, "We could do that." I mean, you might be able to live in a floating city, as in *New York 2140*. But you're not going to be able to move New York up to Albany.

I am interested in this because I think we're in an all-hands-on-deck situation, as I call it. Everything that's ever been proposed for geoengineering is on the table. They're all emergency rescue schemes. Almost all of them are going to be on the table as viable options, and nobody should object to them being discussed. If it happens to be a silver bullet that's run by Silicon Valley billionaires, so what? If it happens to be something that every citizen has to do in their daily life in terms of their own carbon burn, so what? We have to do it.

AD: People will probably first need to feel that these measures, and the personal sacrifices they entail, are really necessary. There is some talk about positive social tipping points. If there ever was a social tipping point, could the experience of the coronavirus pandemic be it? Or will we have to wait for climate disasters on an even greater scale, like the terrible heatwave you describe in your book?

KSR: Yes. I'm thinking of the Green New Deal in the United States, and the European Union's plan for a green recovery from the pandemic. We're in a depression now economically that is real, but that has not yet hit us fully and is not yet spoken of as a depression, even though unemployment levels are the same as during the Great Depression. So there is the possibility of new deals being implemented in a positive government response to address mass suffering.

There is also the Paris Agreement. That was every nation on Earth. That was 2015. It didn't have to happen, and it happened anyway. It might be one of those gestures like the League of Nations, that comes and goes, that dies and doesn't do anything in history. But, on the other hand, it did happen, and it's a possible scaffolding for further good actions.

AD: What about the creation of an international and accountable currency in your novel, an idea proposed by the Ministry for the Future, which is an imagined future organ of the UN?

KSR: This is the creation of a carbon coin, money that gets created and distributed deliberately to Green New

Deal-type projects. Well, it struck me that that might be possible. My hope is that the book will go out there and foster a vision that includes some such programs. So, it's both a utopian novel with a collectivized vision, and also a kind of dramatized policy blueprint, acting out in a way that you can believe in. Never have I tried anything messier. And that's saying a lot, because all of my novels are messy.

AD: Some literary theories say that messiness is really the hallmark of realism. If there's no mess, it's not realistic. It would be like one of those postcards you send from vacation, where everything's perfect and nobody believes it, because it is too stylized, too slick—you just write what you're supposed to write, or worry more about form than truth.

In political parlance, "realism" is often contrasted with optimism or idealism. I saw this contrast taken to the extreme in one of your nonfiction texts, "Is It Too Late?," in the Worldwatch Institute report of 2013. Here, you respond to two questions. To the first, "Is it too late?," you say "No, it is not too late if we do all we can." To the second, "Will we do all we can?," you respond, "No, probably not." How should we relate to this contradiction?

KSR: There is a kind of optimism, which some call "cruel optimism," where we say it will all be fine, while actively taking part in the destruction of the world. In this kind of optimism, we simply divert our gaze from the realm of suffering. But, to turn it around, we are over seven billion people on the planet. A third of these seven billion live a life of suffering, a third are more or less OK, and a third are practically living in utopia already. It is not like we live in a dystopia ruled by a struggle of all against all. There is also a "cruel pessimism," where we say that there is nothing that can be done: the world is doomed, humans are too stupid to survive, such things. We are not really talking about a political conservativism, but rather an extremely limited perspective where one is only concerned with oneself and one's closest family: "As long as we make it through the next 50 years—as long as I, my children, and maybe my grandchildren, are safe—there is no need to think about all the others."

AD: If we try to avoid these suspect forms of optimism and pessimism, we seem to be left with a kind of messy and realist utopianism, like we find in your novels. How can stories like these help us understand and act?

KSR: I mean, I'm not of the belief that any one novel or book can change very much, but you can channel the voices. You can kind of make a document of your time that has an impact on how people see it. So, I do believe novels help to create ideology. I think back to H. G. Wells and his utopian novels—Bretton Woods comes out of them. I think back to Edward Bellamy and *Looking Backward: 2000-1887*, which was a crucial document for the American progressive movement—look at Bellamy Clubs. So, I like that tradition. I want to join that tradition.

AD: You have repeatedly stated that we live in a science fiction story that we all write together. How are we to understand this? Does it mean that things change so fast that we experience a constant future shock? That people are told such crazy stories about what science and technology can bring forth that they lose their capacity to distinguish between fiction and reality, possible and impossible?

Or simply that we all are sucked into one great story about the destiny of our planet?

KSR: It means all these things at once. At the same time, it is a defence for a genre that is dear to me. Many people who don't read it want nothing to do with it. For them, fiction and realism are not to be separated. They don't want to read about non-existent worlds, fantastic phenomena, things they don't already know about from their own experience. So I like to provoke a bit by saying that we already live in a science fiction world, where we make assumptions about the future, and feel hope and fear for what is coming. When we worry about our future, we make personal dystopias, where everything goes wrong. Any positive story we conceive about our own future, even if it is about getting a good job, getting married and having children, is a utopian story.

The future is radically open—so it can be catastrophic or quite good. In this sense, neither optimism nor pessimism right—they are inappropriate emotions for our times. What we need is fear, determination, and courage. Hope is not the same as optimism, the way I see it, but rather something biological. Everything that lives carries it within. Even eating is an act of hope. So attacking hope in some twisted way—saying, "Why do you hope when everything is going to hell?"—is just intellectual posturing. It makes you appear more intelligent and enlightened than the others—as better off, which is again a position filled with secret hopes. Hope is a political position, but also a part of our biological nature—of life itself.

ACKNOWLEDGEMENTS

I would like to give my most heartfelt thanks to all of the participants for giving their time and attention to share their knowledge and perspectives: to Dipesh Chakrabarty, to Jared Diamond, to Sandra Díaz, to Clive Hamilton, to Ursula K. Heise, to Bruno Latour, to Bill McKibben, to Vandana Shiva, warm thanks to Kim Stanley Robinson for an extended and stimulating dialogue over the last years, and to Bernard Stiegler, in memoriam. Special thanks also to Daniel Ross for his generous help along the way, and to Yuk Hui for stimulating exchanges on technology and ecology. I would also like to express my gratitude to three editors in Norway for their great work on the first Norwegian editions: Christian Kjelstrup at Samtiden, whose initiative sparked this series of interviews, Audun Lindholm at Vagant, and Kristian Wikborg Wiese at Spartacus. Great thanks also to Julian Davis for assisting with the English translation, and to everyone at OR Books for making this project happen. Big thanks to my parents, to my brother, and to my wife Annalisa for all of their encouragement along the way–and for sharing my interest in and passion for these topics.